Nurturing Happiness

Natural Ways to Relieve and Prevent Depression

Nurturing Happiness

Natural Ways
to
Relieve and Prevent Depression

By Linda Hoogeveen App

Windmill Press of Alexandria
Alexandria, Virginia

Nurturing Happiness

Natural Ways to Relieve and Prevent Depression

By Linda Hoogeveen App

Note:
This book is intended as a reference volume only, not as a medical manual or guide to self-treatment. The ideas, procedures, and suggestions in this book are not intended to substitute for consultation with your physician or other health care professional. Readers should consult health care professionals before undertaking any major dietary changes, taking any vitamin or dietary supplement, or beginning any exercise regimen.

Published by Windmill Press of Alexandria

First Edition, September, 1997

Library of Congress Catalog Card Number 97-090954

App, Linda Hoogeveen

Nurturing happiness: natural ways to relieve and prevent depression

ISBN 0-9659879-5-7

Printed in the United States of America on recycled paper.

Books are available in quantity discounts. Write to Windmill Press of Alexandria, PO Box 9161, Alexandria, VA 22304, or fax inquiries to (703) 823-7887.

This book is dedicated to
the millions who suffer from depression.

Warning - Disclaimer

This book is designed to provide information regarding the subject matter covered. It is sold with the understanding that the publisher and author are not engaged in rendering medical, psychological, or other professional services. If expert professional assistance is required, the services of a compentent professional should be sought.

Every effort has been made to make this book factually correct. However, there may be mistakes of a typographical or content nature. Therefore, the text should only be used as a general guide.

The purpose of this book is to entertain and educate. The author and Windmill Press of Alexandria shall have neither liability nor responsibility to any person or entity with respect to any loss or damage caused, either directly or indirectly, by the information contained in this book. If you do not wish to be bound by the above, please return this book to the publisher for a full refund.

Acknowledgments

There are many people who deserve my thanks for either direct or indirect input into this book. Their support and encouragement helped me to see this project through to its conclusion.

My friend and literary mentor, Christina Crawford, encouraged me to start my writing project and taught me about writing with a passion and a reason. Her 1978 bestseller, *Mommie Dearest*, helped to break the barrier of silence on the long-denied problem of child abuse in America. She transformed her childhood pain into a life's mission of helping others. Christina's insights into the worlds of writing and publishing, as well as her strong character, have helped guide and inspire me. Her friendship has been, and will continue to be, very precious to me.

My teacher, Paulette R. Bowles, of Nuff Publications, and my fellow writers/classmates in Paulette's course on the book publishing industry all shared their experiences and helped to make publication of this book seem like a real possibility.

Kathy Troutman, author and publisher, shared her professional experiences and provided useful advice.

Friends who provided encouragement while I worked on this book include Dorothy Kuyath, Ava Lee, Nancy Keen, and Alison Bailey Seas. Their friendships over the years have added immeasurably to my life.

Conversations with Shirl Ruffin, a friend and colleague, have contributed to my philosophies on work, career, life, goal-setting, and happiness.

My mother, Phyllis Roberts Hoogeveen, has been a model of inner strength and an example of the power of love. My father, Henry William Hoogeveen, has been a model of financial conservatism and selfless volunteerism. As this book goes to print, they celebrate their fortieth anniversary.

My talented and strong-willed sister, Lisa L. Hauber, provided me with some beautiful reasons to keep going during my own dark days of depression. They are named John, Jena, Jordan, and Jessica.

My twice-widowed aunt, Nell Roberts Johnson, has been an inspiring example of independent womanhood. She has an upbeat attitude, a terrific sense of humor, and a love of family and friends that greatly enriches every life she touches.

My wonderful and loving husband, Steven O. App, has graciously endured all the time I have spent on this book over the last several years. He has constantly encouraged me and prodded me to finish, supplying much-appreciated editorial comments along the way. He has also taught me to be more comfortable with myself, to take more time to enjoy life, and to more clearly see life's gifts and opportunities. I treasure every moment with him.

Finally, I would like to acknowledge the role that God has played in my life. Though I have not attended church regularly since childhood, God has been my constant companion. He has carried me when I could not bear the weight of my troubles, and rescued me in my times of need. His tests have made me a stronger person and His love has made me a happier soul.

Introduction

The incidence of depression has reached epidemic proportions, with tens of millions of Americans taking prescription antidepressant drugs, and millions more in counseling or suffering in silence. In fact, in today's society few of us live a life completely free of depression. Job stress, illness, or the loss of a loved one are all common causes of depression. Many people, living a seemingly perfect life, suffer for reasons they are unable to explain. Regardless of the origin of a person's depression, most sufferers deeply crave relief from this invisible, but very real burden. *Nurturing Happiness* is for sufferers who want simple, natural, cost-effective alternative approaches to: improve their mental health; learn how to become happy again; and maintain that positive state of mind.

This book is empowering, because it explains many of the physiological causes of and cures for depression and shows you exactly what actions you can take on a daily basis to help regain control of your mental health, attitudes, and outlook on life. The alternatives suggested here can help you to take positive actions to provide your mind, body, and spirit with an arsenal of weapons that help fortify you mentally, physically, and spiritually to fight depression when it attacks, and build a foundation for good mental health that reduces the risk of depression in the future. The foundation's building blocks include nutrition, herbs, exercise, and aromatherapy. They also include methods to nurture positive thoughts, create a positive environment, and help you feel happier on a more consistent basis. The recommendations and exercises in the book culminate in the development of your own personally-tailored action plans to relieve depression when it hits and to create a lifestyle that will reduce the risk of future episodes of depression.

Success in overcoming depression is largely dependent on the effort you are willing to expend. If this book has two hundred ideas, and you are only willing to try one or two of them, you are not likely to achieve your optimum levels of happiness and contentment. There are no guarantees in life, except that if you don't try -- you won't succeed. You should be willing to try five or ten ideas, give them a chance to work and then evaluate the results. Next, try another five or ten ideas, and so on. Along the way, you will accumulate a tool kit of things that work, and can discard the things that don't work for you. That is the process of learning which alternatives will help you in your struggle against depression. Once you have done that, you can learn how to maintain a lifestyle that helps you avoid depression, and allows you to keep an "emergency rescue response" plan handy if things take a downturn. It can keep you from panicking.

In the last two years, my research for this book and my own personal experiences have supported the age-old theory of the mind-body-spirit connection. A strong, healthy body and a contented spirit provide a good home for a happy mind. The ideas in this book touch on all three aspects of this triad to help build a strong foundation for a positive mental attitude.

My interest in natural medicines and nutritional healing began almost three years ago. I had spent the first thirty-six years of my life with various and sundry illnesses, allergies, and chronic infections that I constantly treated with doctor visits and pharmaceutical drugs. Quite often, the medical cure for one problem caused another problem, and a vicious cycle ensued. My body, or rather the germs and harmful bacteria in my body, became resistant to antibiotics and soon nothing seemed to help. My digestive problems were such a given part of my life, that I had come to accept them as normal. On vacation in Boston in 1994, my boyfriend (now husband) and I happened upon a store called Hartnett's, next to Harvard University. As I recall, the sign in the window referred to itself as the "un-drug" store. We didn't know it then, but walking through the doors of that store marked a turning point in our lives. Filled with herbal teas for every affliction, rows of nutritional supplements, a juice bar, and a section of reference books and health magazines, it was like no other store we had ever seen. It was totally dedicated to helping people live naturally healthier lives.

I purchased an herbal tea to help relieve symptoms of pre-menstrual syndrome; acidophilus (friendly bacteria) and pau d'arco for recurrent candida infections (a suggestion from the sales clerk); ginko biloba for mental clarity and improved mood; and an herbal sleeping aid. To my amazement, they all worked, and they worked rather quickly. And there were no ill side-effects.

The reference books I bought that day helped lead me further along the path to a natural approach to health. Soon I was building my immune system with odorless garlic pills, green tea, and ginseng. I have strived to eliminate or reduce the toxins in my home, changed my eating habits, and recommitted myself to a regular exercise program. Since that time, my health has improved dramatically. If everyone in my office is sick with the flu and I begin to feel a tickle or soreness in my throat, I take some echinacea root capsules and stay perfectly healthy. The difference in my level of health was nothing short of tremendous. I could leave the house without checking for a full supply of tissues because I no longer had sneezing or severe sinus congestion attacks. I felt free to enjoy life. And I started to notice that I no longer seemed to border on the edge of depression.

In my lifetime, I have had one or two serious episodes of depression. Looking back on those times, it is hard to understand why my life seemed so disappointing. Most who knew me probably thought I was leading a charmed life -- and I was fortunate in many ways, except for a few setbacks of the typical sort (job stress, failed relationships, etc.). But at the time, the hurting was almost unbearable. I did not confide my pain to anyone. I went to work. I attended board meetings, charity events, parties, fundraisers, and family holidays. I know what it is like to suffer in silence. When forcing yourself to smile and say "Hello," is an exhausting effort. There were times I wanted to give up, but I also believed that I could eventually triumph. I worked my way through it with regular exercise, lots of activities, and deep soul-searching with the help of many good books.

My long and desperate struggles lasted up to two years. At the time, I had no idea that there were many more things I could have done to help myself feel better and more ready to face the world each day. I now believe that simple things like improved eating habits, nutritional supplements, and aromatherapy could have pulled me out of the depths much sooner if I had been more informed.

I no longer fear depression. I have beaten it, and I know now how to fight it off if I see it coming again. I have developed a long term strategy that provides for my physical, mental, and spiritual health. All are intricately tied together, and that fact is the basis of the recommendations in this book. Having found relief for myself, it seems selfish not to share what I have learned and make it available to others who are suffering now.

Some of the most wonderful people I have known in my life have suffered from severe depression. Over the last twenty years I have spent countless hours consoling deeply depressed and near-suicidal friends. I have received those three o'clock a.m. phone calls from friends who desperately needed to talk, and stayed overnight in a suicide-watch mode with a friend who was afraid of what he might do if he was left alone. I have phoned the police to request intervention for another friend who had written his suicide note and was moments away from taking his life. I have visited the hospital to see a beautiful, intelligent young woman who had slit her wrists. The night before, she had been with me and several other friends at an after-work event and seemed to have the world by the tail.

They all suffered extreme feelings of sadness and emptiness, because of a relationship break-up, the loss of a job, or even for no apparent reason. It broke my heart to see them in such pain. In the earlier years, all I could offer was friendship and empathy. In recent years, as a result of my new interest in natural health, I have suggested some natural remedies for suffering friends. Initially, I tried writing my suggestions for them on scraps of paper, then typed out lists of foods they should eat, or supplements they could take. But my impact seemed so feeble and insufficient. My lists could only reach the handful of people I knew were suffering, but there are millions more who are searching for relief. The idea for this book was born out of both a sense of obligation and a desire to share. I am glad that it has found its way to you, and I hope you benefit greatly from it.

As this book started to take shape, it became apparent that random, haphazard lists of natural remedies needed to be replaced with a better structure. The search for lasting happiness needed an organized, disciplined approach. While it will not be overtly obvious to the reader, my business background influenced the direction of this book. *Nurturing Happiness* was developed to assist the reader with a logical progression of information gathering, testing, evaluation, planning, and execution. It contains many disguised elements of a business plan. We develop a *mission statement* and perform *goal-setting* when we develop our personal definition of happiness, so that we can target a destination and recognize it when we arrive. We *evaluate existing resources* when we complete an exercise on reasons we already have to be thankful. We perform *cost/benefit analysis* when we test and evaluate numerous suggested remedies. And we perform *crisis management* and *strategic planning* when we develop *short range plans* for intensive therapies to relieve existing depression and *long range plans* for maintenance strategies to prevent future episodes of depression. Finally, we *profit* when we execute our plans and succeed in finding joy in our lives.

This book is titled *Nurturing Happiness* for a reason. It is not called *Instant Happiness*, because there is no way to instantly become happy for a lifetime. Happiness can be deliberately nurtured in your life, much like a rose bush is nurtured in order to blossom and thrive. With proper care, sunshine, water, nutrients, protection from parasites and toxins, and given sufficient time, a rose bush can reach its full potential, thrive, and provide gifts of happiness to those who appreciate its beautiful flowers. The same is true for people. With commitment, time and effort, happiness can thrive in your life. You must be willing to take some responsibility and carry through with your plans on a consistent basis.

Caring for yourself and nurturing your mental health is not a selfish act. It is a necessity. There is no need to be victimized by depression. You have the power to control your reactions to life's difficulties, not to be destroyed or paralyzed by them. You have dreams you want to fulfill and people you want to love. If you are a parent, you surely want to overcome your depression for the sake of your children.

You don't need depression in your life, so let's get on with the business of getting rid of your depression and nurturing your happiness. You may find that the journey will not be as difficult as you thought. You *can* take control of the situation.

As you begin to read this book and work to develop your own tailored action plan for relieving and preventing depression, know that you are in my thoughts and prayers, and that I am wishing you the best in health, happiness, and love.

I would appreciate hearing from readers, and would consider any suggestions for a revised edition of *Nurturing Happiness.* I look forward to hearing from you.

Linda Hoogeveen App
August 1997

c/o Windmill Press of Alexandria
P.O. Box 9161
Alexandria, VA 22304

Table of Contents

Chapter One: Taking Control

Congratulations on your decision to regain control of your life, fend off depression, and begin to actively nurture happiness in your life. I believe that no matter what the cause of your depression, it is within your power to journey out of the land of darkness and despair, and into a world of comfort, serenity, and happiness. The journey is not easy, but by becoming more informed of alternative ways to ease the heavy weight of depression, you can take actions on a daily, weekly, and monthly basis to increase your ability to cope with life's difficulties and ease your depression. There are also actions you can and should take on a regular basis if you are prone to depressive episodes, because they can provide you with a foundation of physical, mental, and spiritual health that could keep depressive episodes at bay, or even eliminate them altogether.

Your body has enormous untapped potential to heal itself. After years of discounting that fact, modern medicine is beginning to accept the idea that nutritional supplements, herbs, prayer, exercise, and other non-medical treatments can positively impact the health of their patients. I have recently become a convert to natural and alternative medicines and healing arts, and have seen a dramatic improvement in my own health. That is proof enough for me, but I strongly encourage you to do your own research because there is so much to learn in this area and the information is becoming readily available.

If there is a bright spot to the AIDS epidemic and the increasing prevalence of cancer, it is that those patients have helped to rejuvenate the interest in alternative medicines because, sadly, modern medicine has so little to offer them. There is still no cure for AIDS, and modern medical cancer treatments are so toxic that they can actually weaken, rather than strengthen, the patient.

Modern medicine's focus is on treatment after the fact, rather than on prevention up-front. Its tools are drugs and surgery (with the associated side-effects and risks), and it does not treat the mind/body/spirit in a holistic way. Natural medicine generally relies on non-patentable treatments and preventive measures such as lifestyle changes, nutrition, herbs, and exercise. Pharmaceutical companies can't make a fortune on herbs the way they can on patented drugs, and surgeons don't make money if they don't operate. So, for reasons of self-interest, the medical-industrial complex is quick to discount the healing successes of natural medicines. Fortunately, some enlightened members of the health care community are beginning to acknowledge and learn about natural and alternative healing, but they are still the exception rather than the rule.

While charges of quackery are often leveled at alternative healers by the established medical profession, I say "Let the results speak for themselves." Every profession has its unethical members, and alternative healing is no different. But the more informed you become as a patient of natural medicine, the less chance there is of your being mislead.

While most people have no trouble determining whether or not they are depressed, here are some common symptoms of depression:

* feelings of worthlessness, guilt, hopelessness, helplessness
* difficulty concentrating
* weight loss or gain
* loss of interest or pleasure in usual activities
* sleeping too much or too little
* thoughts of suicide or death

There are countless causes of depression, and situations that make one person severely depressed may not have any impact on another, and vice versa. There are even times when it is appropriate to feel a certain amount of depression or sadness, such as with the loss of a loved one. But when a reasonable period of time has passed, and it is still difficult to face everyday responsibilities and activities, or you really want to spend the whole day in bed, you have reached a point where you need to regain your emotional balance.

Some people become so severely depressed that they commit suicide, often to the surprise of friends and loved ones who were never given the opportunity to help. People considering suicide need the strength to hang on one more day. Every day presents a world of possibilities. New jobs, new friends, new opportunities, new circumstances, new skills, and a renewed sense of self-worth. Many of us can look back over a one year period of time and think "Wow! A year earlier I never would have dreamed that my life would be so good." But suicidal people can find it difficult to wait for the next sunrise. Some are so depressed they can't stand the thought of surviving another day, much less another week, month, or year.

If you are having recurring thoughts of suicide, I strongly urge you to get professional help immediately from your clergy, physician, therapist, or other health care professional. Having said that -- I know that not everyone needing help will seek it out, but will try to handle it by themselves.

There are numerous reasons why sufferers decide not to seek professional treatment. For some, treatment is not covered by their insurance and they can't afford it on their own. Some may feel that asking for help means they are weak or even crazy.

Others are worried about privacy issues if insurance forms must be filled out and submitted to their employer's personnel office. Some feel that seeking help from a mental health therapist would be detrimental to their career. Working in Washington, DC, I know that many people worry about their security clearances and risk their mental health (by not seeking treatment) for the sake of job security.

Indeed, many of us have filled out employment questionnaires that asked the question "Have you ever been treated for mental illness, including depression?" Knowing you may face answering questions like that does little to encourage people to seek help.

In our nation's not-to-distant past, "troubled" women were shipped to asylums by their husbands, often to spend decades in misery and abuse. Sometimes the "proof" of their "insanity" was that they were kicking and screaming as they were being carted out of their homes by brutish strangers. Even today, if your legal rights or the custody of your children can be taken away by others who deem you incompetent based on your mental health treatment, is there any wonder that troubled souls try to hold everything inside?

I am not trying to discourage anyone from getting professional treatment for depression, in fact I encourage it. I am simply acknowledging the fact that mental health remains a misunderstood topic and many people, for whatever reason, will not seek professional treatment. But they do need help, and that is the purpose of this book. It is my hope that this book will prove useful to those who are under the care of a professional, as well as to those who are trying to deal with their depression on their own terms, and in their own way. It could even be used by someone who is trying to help a friend a family member out of a tough time.

Nurturing Happiness will help you to deal with the immediate time frame, and help answer the question "What can I do *right now* to feel better?" Every chapter contains exercises for you to work through, so you won't finish reading a chapter and say, "That was interesting, but what am I supposed to DO??!!" These exercises will culminate in a personally-tailored action plan that incorporates all of the remedies that have been found to work for you.

There are few new ideas in this book. In fact, many of these healing methods date back thousands of years. But I have pulled together as many "action items" as I could find and tried to explain why this or that action item will help you. The suggestions in this book are relatively inexpensive, and all capitalize on the human body's natural capacity to heal itself, without drugs or invasive medicine.

If you are seeing a doctor for your depression, I would ask you to question how he or she is helping you. Is your doctor giving you an anti-depressant drug and sending you blissfully on your way -- not mentioning any potentially damaging side effects? Is he or she telling you of the important role that nutrition and your environment can play in winning the battle with depression? Does he or she encourage you to face the problems, stresses, or fears that may be the unaddressed root cause of your depression? Does he or she have a plan to help you get over the depression, or plan to keep you on drugs forever? I urge you to ask your doctor to treat the full spectrum of your needs, or at least to help you work with other complimentary approaches to help treat your depression. Most of all, it is important to remember that *you are ultimately responsible for your own happiness* -- not your doctor, your spouse, your child, your boss, your friends, or your parents. You. It's up to you. It will not be easy, but is it within your control.

Tens of millions of Americans regularly take anti-depressant drugs, turning over some of the responsibility for their happiness to the pharmaceutical industry. It is hard to believe that there are that many people with true chemical imbalances, the situation in which anti-depressants are supposedly most appropriate. My bet is that many of those patients and their doctors are looking for a "quick fix" in our instant gratification society. It is certainly quicker to prescribe an anti-depressant than to spend time analyzing the patients' lifestyle, nutritional habits, psychological pressures, or other factors to determine the root cause of the depression. But quick fixes often come with a long term price by masking a symptom rather than treating the underlying causal problem. The long term effects of using these drugs are unknown...I suppose a lot of people will find out the hard way.

This book contains no quick fixes, because I don't believe there are any instant cures that deliver lasting happiness and health. You have to nourish your mind, body, and soul in ways that sustain your mental, physical, and spiritual health. Success is not likely to come overnight; it takes time, effort, and commitment. Improvements will be gradual, and may even go unnoticed until they accumulate to a level that gently nudges you and says "You're feeling better now, aren't you?"

Equilibrium

The natural human state is to be happy and healthy. You deserve health and happiness. It is important to remember that fact. Just as you want health and happiness for your loved ones, they surely want the same for you. I refer to the natural state of health and happiness as equilibrium, and it exists when your body, mind, and spirit are in a state of perfect balance.

Losing Equilibrium

Depression can be described as the loss of mental, emotional equilibrium. This equilibrium can be disrupted by events (loss of a loved one, loss of a job), illness, nutritional deficiencies, food allergies, drug use, or a multitude of other reasons. One event alone may not be enough to bring on depression, but often there is a snowball effect: You lose your job, get out of your routine and forget to exercise, eat junk food because you think it makes you feel better, then gain weight, feel tired, and get depressed.

Figure 1-1 on the next page illustrates the many sources of disruption to our natural state of equilibrium. Think about how many of them, or perhaps other events or circumstances, may be contributing to your own state of imbalance. In the space below, write out some of those things. These thoughts will help you complete other exercises in this book.

Workspace for Personal Thoughts:

Figure 1-1. Numerous Factors Can Contribute To Depression

Natural State of Balance	Affected by	Harmful Factors	Can Result In	Imbalance	Can Lead To	Unnatural State
Equilibrium of Body, Mind, Spirit	⇒	Stressful Events Poor Diet Toxic Environment Illness Financial Difficulties Addictions Job Stress Physical Inactivity	⇒	Disturbed Equilibrium & Compromised Ability to Cope	⇒	Depression

Regaining Equilibrium

Many of the causal factors of depression can be reversed to help treat it. In fact, each contributing factor should be addressed. Poor nutritional habits can be turned around to provide life-sustaining nourishment. Pain from the loss of a spouse can be turned into an appreciation of the time you had together and the things you learned when you were together. Loss of a job can lead to a more meaningful career in a field that you truly love. The hours spent in a lethargic lifestyle (i.e., spent in front of the television) can be gradually turned into the hours dedicated to exercise, hobbies, and helping others.

Additionally, many new approaches can be introduced to your lifestyle that positively impact your mental and physical health. Herbs, teas, aromatherapy, music, colors, relationships, and meditation can all work together in concert to provide a number of equalizing factors to bring balance and happiness back to your world.

This book contains exercises which are intended to help you identify a multitude of factors that can help relieve your depression. Hopefully, you will become more accustomed to "listening to your body" as you note which things do and don't work for you. And, of course, you should talk to your doctor and consider your personal health history, allergies, etc. when deciding which recommendations to try.

Figure 1-2. Numerous Factors Can Help Relieve Depression

Unnatural State	Improved by	Healing Factors	Can Result In	Balancing Effects	Can Lead To	Natural State of Balance
Depression	⇒	Proper Diet Nutritional Supplements Physical Activity Aromatherapy Herbs & Tonics Healthier Environment Inspiring Thoughts Positive Music Worship Helping Others Hobbies/Interests Friends & Family Community Involvement Visualization	⇒	Calmed Disturbances & Improved Ability to Cope	⇒	Equilibrium of Body, Mind, Spirit

Figure 1-2 illustrates some of the numerous ways we can respond to depression to help regain our equilibrium. This book will focus on the stabilizing factors represented in *Figure 1-2*. We will explore ways to strengthen our bodies, nourish our hearts, and enrich our minds. Each will reinforce the other as we nurture happiness in our lives.

Five Steps to Balance

There are five basic steps to regaining balance of mind, body, and spirit. You are in control at each step in the process, and your actions will determine your degree of success.

1. Acknowledge your state of imbalance.

2. Seek out help from friends, books, and professionals.

3. Make plans to nurture your spirit, body, and mind.

4. Stay committed to your plans.

5. Understand that achieving balance (happiness) will take time and effort.

Your reading of this book indicates that you have taken the first step of recognizing that you have a problem, and the second step of seeking out help. As you work through the exercises in this book, you will be accomplishing the third step of formulating your plans to nurture your mind, body, and spirit. The fourth step calls for you to stay committed to your plans, not just in the short term to solve the current crisis, but for a lifetime. You should do everything in your power to prevent depression in the future. After you have won your current battle with depression, you should maintain a lifestyle that nurtures your mental health. Lastly, as you work you way through any period of depression, be patient. Understand that it is a phenomenon that will pass with time and with the help of your nurturing efforts. Life will not always be easy and we all have to learn to cope with the difficulties that come our way.

Your Commitment to Try

Here, at the beginning of this book, you should look into your heart and ask yourself how committed you are to really trying alternative methods of relieving your depression. *A high level of commitment is crucial to your success.* If you expect reading this book to help you feel better, you are not being realistic unless you are also willing to try some recommendations and change some aspects of your life, such as your eating habits, your activity level, and your environment, to name just a few things. This book will help you figure out what those changes should be, if you work through the exercises and are willing to keep an open mind.

You are about to encounter the first of many exercises in this book. You will want to get a pen or pencil, and be prepared to spend five minutes answering the questions in the exercise. The purpose of *Exercise 1-1* is to determine how hard you are willing to work to feel good on a consistent basis. You should be willing to try some ideas that you may find new or unusual, such as aromatherapy, visualization, and music therapy. Think through the questions in *Exercise 1-1*, and make a realistic evaluation of your commitment level. On a scale of 0 to 10 (zero = not at all willing to try; 10 = very willing to make a continuous commitment).

Exercise 1-1.

How Committed Am I?

How committed am I to taking action to feel better?

How willing am I to change my diet?

How willing am I to try nutritional supplements?

How willing am I to try herbal supplements and teas?

How willing am I to make time for nature in my life?

How willing am I to get into a regular exercise routine?

Hopefully, this exercise has helped you focus and commit to a certain level of dedication to this project. There are many other things that this book will suggest you try, beyond those listed in *Exercise 1-1*. The purpose of that exercise was to simply persuade you to commit to trying an assortment of remedies which may work for you. The only way to determine what works for you is to actually test some of them and evaluate the results.

Reality Check

Though depression can make you feel very isolated, the truth is that there are many people in the same boat, and self-pity may be the only pity you get. It is important to do a reality check, to see if things are as bad as you think they are. Perhaps things are not as hopeless as they seem.

One of the first steps in being happy is to appreciate the things that you already have and may be taking for granted. Can you walk? Can you communicate with others? Do you have enough to eat? Is your family healthy? Do you have a roof over your head? Does someone love you? Do you have others to love? Are you educated? Are you employed? Take a few minutes and complete the *Exercise 1-2*. Do not stop at one-word responses. Write as much as you can in each space. Realizing how much you have to be thankful for should make your heart feel a little happier.

Exercise 1-2.

"Giving Thanks" Exercise

I am thankful that I am physically able to:

I am thankful because my spirit is:

I am thankful for my family because:

I am thankful for my freedom to:

I am thankful because my home is:

I am thankful because my friends are:

I am thankful for my past experiences in:

I am thankful because I have the skills to:

I am thankful for my education in:

I am thankful for my opportunities to:

I am thankful because my community is:

I am thankful because my country is:

I am thankful because the world is:

I am thankful for many other things, such as:

The previous exercise may help you to realize that you have already attained a great many things that form a foundation for happiness. Hopefully, working through the statements in that exercise has helped to lift your spirits a little.

Defining Happiness

Our goal should be to go beyond just "not being so depressed anymore," but expand to "being happy and content on a more consistent basis." Perhaps we need to redefine happiness. If we think we cannot be happy unless we are in a constant state of total bliss, then we have wildly unrealistic expectations for our lives because we have not properly defined happiness. If the choice you give yourself is either "total bliss" or unhappiness, you are likely to be unhappy most of the time.

How do you define happiness? Answer the following questions in *Exercise 1-3*, and take as long as you need to answer them.

Exercise 1-3.

Identifying Happiness

How do you define happiness?

What will your life be like when you are happy?

What kind of people will be in your life?

Where will you live?

How will you spend your time?

What is (or would you like to be) your mission in life?

Exercise 1-4 will help to identify some reasons for your depression and possible responses to the situations. It is best to be as specific as possible when identifying the problem in the first column, so the solution in the second column becomes more obvious.

You may have three comments on your job, and four on your relationships. For example, your first instinct may be to write "I hate my job" in the first column and "Get new job" in the second column. But be more specific. What exactly do you hate about this job? Do you enjoy the work, but find your co-workers or boss to be obnoxious and inconsiderate? Do you enjoy your co-workers, but hate the work itself or the long hours? Do you believe in the mission of your organization, or do you hate what it stands for? If you can be very specific about what is eating at you, it is easier to face the issue and work toward some kind of resolution.

On a more personal level, you may be dissatisfied with a relationship. The problem may not be your partner, but perhaps the poor communication or behavior patterns that have developed between you and your partner that you both keep repeating with dissatisfying results. Once you have specifically identified the problem, you may realize you need a new pattern, not a new partner.

In the first column in *Exercise 1-4* ("Why?"), list 3 or 4 reasons why you think you are depressed. In the second column ("Better If ..."), write down what it would take to make you feel better if or when something else happens to change the situation. In the third column ("I Could ..."), write down what actions you could take to make the events that are listed in the second column actually happen. You may want to complete this exercise on a larger sheet of paper.

Exercise 1-4.

❦ What's Got You Down? ❦

Why?	Better If...	I Could...

Fear may also be contributing to your depression. If your thoughts are preoccupied with worry about things that may or many not ever happen, you are wasting valuable energy. Use *Exercise 1-5* to identify any unreasonable fears you may have. Answer the series of questions in *Exercise 1-5* for every major fear that you have.

Exercise 1-5

❦ Fear Identification ❦

1. What do you fear?

2. What is the worst thing that could happen?

3. How would you deal with that worst possible scenario? (List several alternatives.)

4. Is there anything you can do to prevent your worse fear from happening? If yes, list here.

Having completed the *Exercises 1-4* and *1-5* on what is making you depressed, spend some time evaluating your answers. Looking at your problems in black and white -- do they still seem as serious? My bet is that once all your problems are broken down into segments, you can start to grasp the manageability of the situation. When addressed one piece at a time, you may be able to see that the problems are not insurmountable. There may be things you can do in the short term to minimize the effects of those problems, while make long term plans to eliminate the problems.

In *Exercise 1-6*, you will make use of your efforts in *Exercises 1-4* and *1-5*. You will identify actions you can take in the short term to relieve some of your depression and anxiety.

Exercise 1-6.

❦ Taking Some Action ❦

1. Promise yourself to take two action steps this week to implement some of the items you listed in your third column of *Exercise 1-4*. Identify those two action steps here.

2. Plan a timetable for implementing the other items from the third column in *Exercise 1-4* and the fourth question in *Exercise 1-5*.

Chapter One was successful if it convinced you of your power to control your reaction to depression. No one is guaranteed an easy life, and we all have to learn how to appreciate our gifts and deal with our adversities. In fact, suffering through some tough times can really make you appreciate the good times even more. Control over depression also involves building physical and mental strength and stamina. In Chapter Two, we will address one of the most fundamental aspects of good physical and mental health: nutrition.

Note: The information presented in this book is for general reference only. You should consult with your health care professional before making any dietary changes, taking any supplements, or beginning any exercise regimen. You may have allergies or other health concerns which might preclude you from trying some of the recommendations in this book. And be sure to use your common sense.

Chapter Two: Developing a Nutritional Strategy

It may surprise you to know the full extent to which nutrition plays a role in maintaining a positive mental outlook and feeling good in general. It may even surprise some doctors, since few receive formal training in nutrition in medical school. Depression has been linked to deficiencies in several nutrients, and this knowledge can be useful in fighting depression, because nutritional deficiencies are easily cured through diet and dietary supplements. Therefore, it is possible to both treat and prevent depression with good nutrition. Learning which kinds of food and nutritional supplements help stave off depression, is one of the most important strategies to learn in your efforts to nurture happiness in your life.

The more you learn about the importance of good nutrition, the more obvious it becomes that treatment with antidepressant pharmaceutical drugs may be masking simple nutritional deficiencies. In this chapter, we will explore the numerous nutritional alternatives available to us in fending off bouts of depression. We will only cover highlights here. I strongly encourage readers to refer to other authoritative literature such as *The Doctor's Complete Guide to Vitamins and Minerals* by Mary Dan Eades, M.D; *Prescription for Nutritional Healing* by James F. Balch, M.D. and Phyllis A. Balch, C.N.C.; and the

Complete Guide to Vitamins, Minerals & Supplements by H. Winter Griffith, M.D.

Foods today may not be as rich in vitamins and other nutrients as they had been in decades past because of the over-use of nutrient-depleted topsoil in our nation's farming regions. Though farmers use fertilizers to help the foods grow, most fertilizers are not composed of the full range of nutrients our bodies need. Unless you shop exclusively for organically-grown produce and meats, you really can't rely solely on a well-planned diet to meet all your nutritional needs. This means that we must try harder than our grandparents had to in order to ensure a nutrition-rich diet. In addition to the fact that food crops today have fewer nutrients, our nation's eating habits have deteriorated over the years. Most diets today are high in fats, sugars, and processed foods (where the nutrients have been processed-out). Instead, we should be eating more fresh fruits, vegetables, and whole grains. We should eat dairy products and meats far less frequently (because of the antibiotics, steroids, and pesticides that are in livestock feed), and we should not eat any fried foods.

I have recently discovered the writings of John Robbins, who argues for healthier diets and explains how our nation's collective eating habits (high in meat proteins) can harm the environment. I had never made the connection before, but his writing lovingly and eloquently tells the tale, and I encourage you to read *Diet for a New America*. As I write this section of the book, I am six months into my New Year's resolution to become a vegetarian, for both personal health and ethical reasons (the cruel treatment of animals - - not just at their death, but throughout their lives - - and the damage to the environment caused by the production of beef and other meats). I tell you this because I feel compelled to preach the benefits of a vegetarian diet. However, I am not sure if I will be able to maintain such a diet myself, though it has been easier than I expected. I encourage you to pursue vegetarianism, but I will not yet hold myself up as a shining example. Since most readers are probably not vegetarians, meat and dairy sources of nutrients will be listed where appropriate.

NUTRITION AND SUPPLEMENTS

Can your food effect your mood? Could relief from depression be as simple as taking a pill? Are there safe, non-habit forming, non-"drug" pills available to the general public that can help lift you out of the doldrums? The answer to those questions is a qualified "Yes." There are foods and non-prescription, inexpensive, readily-available, effective nutritional supplements that have been shown to help relieve symptoms of depression.

Talk to your health care practitioner about nutritional therapy and getting tested for nutritional deficiencies. If you can't or won't do that, review your dietary intake and see if you are deficient in certain kinds of nutrients. If you are currently under a doctor's care and are taking antidepressant drugs, ask your doctor to consider vitamin therapy as well.

In some cases, mild depression can be brought on by a diet low in certain vitamins or minerals. Your brain needs certain chemicals found in vitamins and other nutrients in order to work effectively. If you don't provide them, is it any wonder when your brain is not operating at peak performance? Additionally, there are some natural herbal substances that have been proven to help relieve symptoms of depression. These vitamins, minerals, and other substances can be found in tablet or capsule form, the easiest way to get those things into your diet.

To depression at bay, diets should have sufficient levels of vitamins B and C, Iron, Biotin, and certain amino acids. Fortunately, the market is now flooded with nutrition supplements that can easily be found at your local health food store, drugstore, or through mail-order.

B Vitamins

B vitamins are real "brain vitamins," and are vital to the healthy functioning of the human brain. Deficiencies in B vitamins cause low levels of the brain chemical serotonin, which is important in achieving happy and contented moods. Personally, I have also noticed a distinct increase in mental alertness and energy when I increased my intake of B vitamins.

The two most important B vitamins used in combating depression are B6 and B12. Vitamin B12 deficiencies have been linked to depression, and Vitamin B6 has been shown to correct depression in patients. Therefore, it is important to insure that your diet has sufficient levels of these B vitamins. Even if our diets include enough B vitamins, lifestyle choices can lower the level of B vitamins in our system. Oral contraceptives, antacids, laxatives, stress, smoking, alcohol, and high-fiber diets can all contribute to vitamin B12 deficiencies. (High fiber diets are healthy, but just be aware of the impact on B12 nutrients.) If your lifestyle is contributing to a vitamin B deficiency, you'll need to get more than the minimum Recommended Daily Allowance (RDA) levels established by the U.S. Food and Drug Administration.

Vitamin B6 (Pyridoxine) is available in tablet form. A recommended dosage for most adults is 10-25 mg per day. But studies have shown that depressed women who took oral contraceptives were able to alleviate the depression by taking vitamin B6 in supplemental doses of 25 - 50 mg per day. Vitamin B6 can be found in the following foods: liver, soybeans, bananas, beef, chicken, pork, tuna, walnuts, peanuts, and avocados.

Vitamin B12 (Cobalamin) is absorbed differently than other vitamins. Because the hydrochloric acid in the stomach can destroy much of the vitamin B12 before it gets to your system, many doctors recommend B12 injections. Another alternative is taking the vitamin in sublingual form -- drops taken below the tongue. Some chiropractors are also licensed to give B12 injections. Check with your health care practitioner if you are interested in B12 injections. B12 vitamins are also available in tablet form, often with other vitamins in a B-complex form. B12 is such a potent vitamin that it is measured in micrograms rather than milligrams. The RDA for adult men and women is 2 to 3 micrograms per day. B12 is only found in foods from animal sources, rather than plants. Higher levels of B12 are found in the organ meats (liver and kidney) and bivalve mollusks (oysters and clams). Lesser amounts can be found in crab, salmon, beef, chicken, pork, tuna, swordfish, lobster, scallops, and flounder.

Biotin is also a member of the B vitamin group. Deficiencies in biotin are rare, but it can be a contributing factor to depression. The recommended dosage is 100 to 200 micrograms a day. But if you are fighting off depression, try adding 300 micrograms to your daily diet for 4-6 weeks and see if there is any improvement. Take it with food to decrease the possibility of stomach irritation.

Biotin is produced by friendly intestinal bacteria and is found in the following foods: liver, peas, tuna, soy flour, cereal, and yeast. Antibiotics and alcohol consumption can interfere with the production of biotin.

Vitamin C

A deficiency of vitamin C (Ascorbic Acid) is one of the earliest detectable symptoms of depression. In fact, even a mild deficiency can lead to depression. Vitamin C is also needed by the body's immune system to help ward off illnesses. Vitamin C must be consumed every day because it cannot be stored by the body since it is water-soluble. Excess amounts that the body does not use in a day are excreted in urine. Aspirin and oral contraceptives inhibit the absorption of vitamin C, so take this information into consideration when evaluating your need for nutritional supplements.

The RDA for vitamin C is 60 mg per day, but most of my research recommends much higher levels (2,000 to 5,000 mg per day) for optimal health and to fight depression. Ironically, higher doses of vitamin C inhibit the body's ability to absorb vitamin B12. Since both vitamins are important in fighting depression, you must achieve a delicate balance between the two. It may be best to take the vitamins at different times of day to help absorption of each.

It may be best to take B vitamin supplements in the morning, since they are so mentally refreshing. In fact, I sometimes have difficulty sleeping if I take B vitamins at night because my mind becomes so alert that I don't feel like sleeping anymore. The vitamin C supplements can be taken at night, and can help strengthen your immune system while you rest.

Foods containing high levels of vitamin C include: citrus fruits, strawberries, melons, tomatoes, leafy green vegetables, and broccoli.

Minerals

Iron is the mineral most closely associated with depression treatment. An iron deficiency has been shown to cause depression and an inability to concentrate. Iron can be taken in tablet form and a recommended dosage is 10 mg per day for men and 18 mg per day for women. It is best to have a doctor confirm the presence of an iron deficiency, because there are problems associated with having too much iron in your diet. Read the label of iron products, and pick products with "elemental" iron. Your iron supplement should also contain folic acid.

Iron can, unfortunately, cause constipation, so you may want to look for tablets with stool softeners among the ingredients. Iron should be taken at the same time as vitamin C, which not only aids in iron absorption, but also helps prevent constipation. (Remember, don't take laxatives because they will interfere with vitamin B12 absorption.) Iron should not be taken along with vitamin E, calcium supplements, or caffeine because they will interfere with the absorption and assimilation of iron. Food sources of iron include liver, beef, veal, chicken, pork, clams, fish, spinach, asparagus, prunes, and raisins.

Calcium is known to have a calming effect and to be important to the nervous system. Most people know that calcium is found in dairy products such as milk and cheese. It is also found in seafood, green leafy vegetables, figs, prunes, and tofu. If you know your diet is falling short on calcium intake, a recommended supplemental dosage is 1,500 mg daily. It will be more effective if taken in smaller doses spread throughout the day and at bedtime, when it can also help promote sound sleep. However, calcium supplements should not be taken by individuals with kidney problems.

Magnesium is also important to the nervous system. A deficiency can cause nervousness and irritability. Dietary supplements of magnesium help prevent depression, and aid in the uptake of calcium. The use of alcohol increases the body's need for magnesium. Like calcium, magnesium is found in dairy products, green leafy vegetables, and seafood. It is also found in apples, bananas, figs, garlic, nuts, peaches, and whole grains. If taken as a dietary supplement, the recommended dosage is 1,000 mg daily.

Chromium aids the body's metabolism, helping to mobilize fats for energy. It also helps to stablize blood sugar levels. Chromium can be found in beer, brown rice, cheese, corn, chicken, mushrooms, and potatoes. As a supplement, 300 mg daily is recommended.

Amino Acids

L-Glutamine. Glutamine is a building block of protein, and assists in the proper functioning of the brain. It has also become important in the treatment of alcoholism because its helps curb the cravings for alcohol.

L-Phenylalanine. Phenylalanine produces neurotransmitters in the brain. As a result, there are several benefits to this amino acid. It is often used to treat depression because of its ability to elevate moods. It also aids in memory and learning, and can decrease the pain of migraine headaches, menstruation, and even arthritis. Apparently, it is important to strike a delicate balance with this amino acid because low levels of it are found in depressed patients, but high levels may be found in schizophrenic patients. L-Phenylalanine is found in chocolate and cow's milk. Caution: Phenylalanine should not be taken as a supplement by pregnant women, or those who suffer from high blood pressure, skin cancer, or anxiety attacks.

L-Tryptophan. Tryptophan is one of the most important nutrients to be considered in the treatment of depression While it has many other functions, Tryptophan has an important role in facilitating the transmission of nerve impulses within the brain and nervous system by forming compounds called "neurotransmitters." One vital neurotransmitter is serotonin, which helps relieve depression and is responsible for normal sleep. Tryptophan is especially effective at producing serotonin, and thus is a key nutrient in the diet. It can be an effective sleep aid, can suppress appetite, and act as an anti-depressant.

Tryptophan is found in bananas, dried dates, fish, turkey, peanuts, wheat germ, eggs, cottage cheese, avocados, pork, spirulina (algae), and almonds.

Until 1989, Tryptophan was available as a dietary supplement in the United States and was widely used as a natural, low-cost, effective, and safe treatment for depression. Unfortunately, a contaminated batch of Tryptophan from an Asian manufacturer caused some serious health problems for a number of consumers. Rather than recall the product, such as was done with contaminated Tylenol, the sale of Tryptophan as a dietary food supplement in the U.S. has been banned indefinitely (with or without a prescription).

Coincidentally, the "miracle drug" Prozac was introduced to the U.S. market shortly after Tryptophan was taken off the market. Prozac also helps create serotonin - - at a higher price and with notable side effects.

❧A Word About Pharmaceutical Antidepressants

Many people are finding relief from depression with pharmaceutical antidepressants. While these drugs may help relieve the symptoms of depression, the drugs can also have some very serious side effects. If you need more information about antidepressants, I strongly urge you to read *Talking Back to Prozac*, by Peter R. Breggin, M.D. and Ginger Ross Breggin, St. Martin's Paperbacks, 1994.

L-Tyrosine. A lack of Tyrosine can cause a deficiency of the hormone norephinephrine in the brain. This can result in mood disorders and depression. Tyrosine is also involved in the production of epinephrine and dopamine, which affect impulse transmissions in the brain. Tyrosine is used in the treatment of depression, anxiety, headaches, and allergies. Tyrosine can be found naturally in almonds, avocados, bananas, peanuts, and pumpkin seeds.

Nature's Whole Food

You may be wondering if there is any one food that can boast a complete line-up of required nutrients. The closest thing I have been able to find is from an unlikely source: algae. This simple food source packs a nutritional wallop. My husband and I have been taking algae in capsule form for almost three years, and have noticed great benefits. We have fewer cravings between meals, because our bodies are not calling for missing nutrients. We are more mentally alert because our brains have the fuel they need to work at their peak. And though we are approaching middle age, we haven't slowed down one bit when it comes to exercise and physical endurance because this "food" contains the anti-oxidants that we need to keep our bodies from aging before their time.

We tried a few of the less expensive retail algae products, but have settled on the higher-priced mail order Super Blue Green™ algae produced by Cell Tech in Klamath Falls, Oregon. It's worth the additional investment. If you would like to call for more information, Cell Tech's phone number is (800) 800-1300. I'll tell you up front that it is a multi-level marketing program. If you sign up to be a distributor (a one-time charge of a few extra dollars), you will pay lower prices for all the products you order in the future. They will probably ask you for a "sponsor" name when you call. Tell 'em Steven O. App sent you.

Strategic Nutrition: A Personal Log

I encourage you to try various nutritional supplements and foods to see if they impact your depression. As you try them, keep track of the usage duration and its results in *Exercise 2-1* and *2-2*. In the last column of both exercises, register a yes or no, for whether or not you will add each nutritional supplement or food to your personal maintenance plan.

Exercise 2-1

Personal Nutritional Supplements Log

Nutrient	Date/Duration	Good Results?
B6		
B12		
Biotin		
Vitamin C		
Iron		
Calcium		
Magnesium		
Chromium		
Selenium		
Zinc		
L-Glutamine		
L-Phenylalanine		
L-Tryptophan		
L-Tyrosine		

Exercise 2-2

❦ Personal Nutritional Food Log ❦

Food	Date/Duration	Good Results?

Over the years I have learned that foods have an immediate impact on how I feel. Though I may crave a fast food burger and fries, I know that all of that grease and fat really does a number on my digestive system, and makes my body feel clogged, poisoned, heavier, and slower. In contrast, a fresh spinach salad with walnuts and a raspberry vinaigrette dressing fills me up, yet my body feels light and fresh and healthy. *When it is time to eat a meal, focus on how you want to feel afterward, rather than on what you want to taste.* Before long, you'll be craving the healthier foods because of your positive associations between healthy food and feeling good.

Nutritional Planning

Proper nutrition is one key way to nurture a positive mental attitude. Vitamins, minerals, and amino acids play an important role in the proper functioning of the brain and in maintaining elevated moods. Fortunately they are all readily available as nutritional supplements without a prescription, except for tryptophan. It is therefore important to include foods high in Tryptophan in your diet.

> Note: The quality of nutritional supplements varies, depending on the manufacturer. Seek out reputable brands.

Figure 2-1 serves to give you a few ideas on menu planning to help counter depression. Here are a few helpful hints:

* Try to eat only organically grown foods.

* Stop eating when you are no longer hungry, rather than when full.

* Don't overcook vegetables; cooking kills nutrients.

* Find great-tasting, low-fat salad dressings, so you will look forward to having salads.

Figure 2-1

Menu Items to Mix and Match
Breakfast Cantaloupe Oranges Grapefruit Strawberries Plain or vanilla yogurt Rose hips tea Ginseng tea
Lunch Caesar salad Garden salad with tomato Spinach salad Vegetable juice Tuna or chicken salad on whole wheat Green tea
Snacks Bananas Oranges Peaches Nuts (almonds, peanuts) Prunes/Raisins Figs (or fig cookies) Pumpkin seeds

Figure 2-1, Continued

Menu Items to Mix and Match Continued
Dinner Beef liver Turkey Beef Chicken Pork Tuna Flounder Salmon Lobster Swordfish Soy Brown rice Potatoes Green leafy vegetables Broccoli Sweet potatoes or yams

Now that you have some ideas for better nutrition, *Exercise 2-3* will help you plan your meals. It is important to plan meals ahead so that you have the right groceries in the house or so that you plan your restaurant menu choices to the fullest extent possible.

Exercise 2-3

❦ Planning to Eat Right ❦

1. Look through books and magazines for delicious, healthy recipes.

2. Make your own recipe collection in a scrapbook or in recipe card form. Cut out magazine pictures that make health eating look delicious.

3. Plan a day's menu for when you will need emergency nutritional support.

4. Decide what eating habits you will adopt.

    a. What will you add to your diet?

    b. What will you delete from your diet?

Eating the proper nutritious foods and taking any needed supplements can have a dramatic impact on your mental attitude. There are other plant-derived products on the market that can also help improve your mood. Chapters Three and Four will discuss the use of nature's herbs, essences, oils, and teas to assist you in relieving depression and regaining a positive outlook on life.

Chapter Three: Supplementing Your Diet With Herbs and Other Natural Substances

A few years ago, talk of using medicinal herbs was considered to be something that hippies and witchdoctors did, but it certainly was not mainstream. Americans today are beginning to catch up with other nations that use healing herbs and other alternative medicines as routine practice, often in conjunction with modern medicine, and achieving high levels of health at a much lower cost. We have begun to find answers in alternative medicines for both treatment and prevention, where modern medicine's reliance on high technology and pharmaceutical drugs (and their requisite side-effects) has not produced the expected results in spite of its high costs.

The shamans, herbalists, midwives, and other natural healers have relied upon herbs for thousands of years to help their patients overcome illnesses of all types, and I wonder if the human race could have survived without these early medicines. Indeed, many modern medicines got their origins from plants used in early medicines. Scientists are now beginning to seriously study the potential of plants to heal, and many efforts to help save the earth's rainforests are partly based on the potential medicinal benefits that might be derived from the thousands of species of plants that we have yet to catalog.

This chapter focuses on a few of the more commonly used herbs and other natural substances that have great potential for relieving or alleviating depression. You will want to tailor your use of these herbs to your specific situation. For example, if you are lethargic and tired, ginseng would be appropriate to try because of its energizing properties. But if you are depressed due to stress and a primary symptom is nervousness, you would probably want to try valerian, because of its calming effect. If your work or lifestyle keeps you outdoors in sunlight, you'll want to avoid St. Johns Wort. I've tried to give you a range of options, and you can try what is most appropriate for you. First we will discuss supplements (available in capsule or tablet form, usually), and then herbal teas.

Herbal Supplements for Depression

Herbal supplements (some called tonics) are becoming extremely popular, and can even be found in mainstream pharmacies. Capsules and tablets provide a very convenient way to add herbal therapy to your list of ways to relieve and prevent depression.

Ginseng

There are several types of Ginseng that are becoming popular in mainstream America for various health reasons. They include Korean, Chinese, American, and Siberian Ginseng.

Siberian ginseng is the most effective type of Ginseng in fighting depression, though it is best used as a preventative measure rather than a cure after an onset of depression. Siberian Ginseng is made from the root of the Siberian Ginseng plant, *Eleutherococcos senticosus.* Recommended dosage is 1/2 gram to 3 grams daily. Children would take smaller doses, and it is best to check with a pediatrician for a recommended dosage.

Research has documented many benefits of Siberian Ginseng. It:

* Increases energy and endurance
* Improves performance
* Protects against excessive heat or cold
* Protects against viral and microbial infection
* Acts as a detoxifier
* Provides a sense of well-being and more joy in life
* Improves the quality of sleep, but is not sleep-inducing
* Helps fight possible damage from exposure to radiation (x-rays, computer screens, microwaves, and televisions)

Chinese (panax) ginseng is effective in helping the body cope with stress, helps provide an improved sense of well-being, and improves mental functioning. It should be avoided by high blood pressure patients.

Ginseng is becoming very popular in the U.S. today. Not only are ginseng supplements more readily available in neighborhood pharmacies (and, of course, health food stores), but ginseng is also beginning to be more popular in teas and foods. Since it tends to be energizing, it is probably best to take in the morning. You can also take it at intervals throughout the day, but should stop taking it in the evening hours so that you sleep well at bedtime. Check with your health care practitioner to see if you should take ginseng during pregnancy.

Ginko Biloba

Ginko Biloba may be the world's best-selling over-the-counter product. Used in Chinese medicine for thousands of years, today it is used widely in Europe and Asia. Its effectiveness has been substantiated in scientific tests, and the volume of product sales is testament to the loyalty of its users. It is made from the leaves of the ginko biloba tree.

Ginko biloba extract improves mental alertness and boosts memory by increasing the flow of blood to the brain. It helps to alleviate depression and headaches. It seems to help normalize existing disturbances in the brain's neurotransmitters and their receptors. It also acts as an anti-oxidant, fighting the damage of "free radicals" to the membranes in our bodies.

If you have noticed that you are not as mentally sharp as you were a few years ago, you may have another reason to try ginko. You may notice an immediate effect on your mental alertness, if not your depression. By the way, it is also proven to have some positive effects with Alzheimer's Disease, asthma, and tinnitus patients.

When buying ginko biloba, look for a 24% standardized extract of the flavonoid glycosides, which ensures standardized potency in each pill. A generally recommended dosage is 40 mg three times per day. One reputable name brand is GinkGold, and it is becoming readily available in pharmacies and health food and nutrition stores. There are a few potential side effects, such as gastrointestinal upset or headaches. Some people have suffered allergic reactions to the fruit pulp. *If you have a bad reaction to this or any other recommendation in this book, simply stop following the recommendation.*

St. Johns Wort

St. Johns Wort (hypercium perforatum) is a natural anti-depressant, and is most commonly used for this purpose, though it has been used as a folk remedy for centuries to treat a wide variety of problems. It acts as a "mood lightener," and can provide a sense of well-being, and a calming effect. Prolonged use is discouraged because it has been known to cause a sensitivity to light. It is also a mild diuretic, and can help to relieve menstrual cramping. St. Johns Wort is used more commonly in Europe than in the US, but recent mainstream news stories touting its benefits may increase usage. A recommended dosage for an adult is 250 mg daily of the standardized .14% (0.35 mg) hypercin extract, or 4 grams of the dried herb.

Valerian

The best known insomnia herb, Valerian (Valeriana officinalis) may also be appropriate for treating certain symptoms of depression such as nervousness and sleeplessness. It can help you get the sleep you may be needing. The valerian plant was used hundreds of years ago by Native Americans, who ate the root and flowers in raw form or ground it into flour. Originally an ingredient in the potent and popular pharmaceutical drug Valium, the valerian root effectively calms the central nervous system. It has also been shown to help headaches, nervous stomach, irritable bowel, stomach cramps and menstrual cramps.

The valerian root herb is reported to be safe to take during pregnancy and breast-feeding (but you should check with your doctor), and does not produce a morning-after hangover effect like most over-the-counter sleeping pills. As an asthmatic, I know that I have a bad respiratory reaction when I take over-the counter sleeping pills, yet I have never had a problem with valerian. It is a gentle-acting herb that does not leave me groggy the next day. I always awaken refreshed and alert. The recommended dosage for insomnia is 400 to 450 milligrams taken just before bedtime. It has a rather pungent aroma, but don't let that discourage you from taking this useful herb if you think you may need it. Smaller doses can be used during the day to calm nervousness and stress.

Evening Primrose

Evening Primrose (oenothera biennis) is most often used to treat coughs due to colds, but it has also been used in the treatment of depression. Its stimulating effects on the spleen and liver may help flush toxins out of the body.

Sage

Sage has been used to treat nervous conditions including depression, *but extended use can cause poisoning symptoms. Use sage only for short periods of time.* Sage is more commonly used to treat night sweats, because it reduces perspiration. It is also used for digestive and respiratory ailments. Sage should not be used at all by pregnant women.

Make sage tea by steeping two teaspoons of sage leaves in a cup of water. Drink one tablespoonful at a time throughout the day.

Other Immune System Builders

The three following substances are not being recommended because of any direct link to relieving depression, but purely as additional information on simple, effective ways to help build your immune system. They are presented here because sufferers of depression may have reduced immune strength, and may have a tendency to catch colds or other minor illnesses.

Garlic. For thousands of years, healers have recognized garlic as a natural wonder drug. Worldwide research on garlic has shown it to have numerous healing qualities such as its ability to: prevent cancer, lower cholesterol, reduce blood pressure, provide energy, and resist colds. Side effects (such as diarrhea, heartburn, rapid pulse) generally occur only after long term consumption of large doses. There is no need to worry about garlic-breath, because garlic tablets and capsules are available in odorless form. It can be taken daily in safe doses and is a super immune system builder.

Echinacea. Echinacea is commonly used by natural medicine patients to help fend off colds and flu. It should be used for short term duration so as not to reduce its effectiveness when it is needed. I use it whenever I feel a cold coming on, and now lots of my friends are true believers, too. This herb is also going mainstream, and can often be found at drugstores.

Bee Pollen. Bee pollen is known for its energizing effect. It is rich in many nutrients, including amino acids, calcium, carotene, iron, magnesium, B complex, and vitamin C. Bee pollen can be found in capsule form or in a honey-like substance, that can be used in teas for sweetener. Some people are allergic to bee pollen. If you have reason to believe you may be among that group, either avoid bee pollen altogether or try it first in tiny doses and discontinue if any allergic reactions occur.

Avoid During Pregnancy

Some (but certainly not all) herbs should be avoided during pregnancy, and I have noted that fact where those herbs are discussed in this book. Just to be on the safe side, I am providing a list of those herbs, based upon information that I happened upon while researching this book. There is no guarantee that this list is complete, but since many readers may be pregnant, I thought it might be useful to pass this information along. Pregnant women should consult their health care practitioner before using any herbs.

During pregnancy, the following herbs should be avoided: dong qui, poke, cayenne, pennyroyal, ephedra (also known as mu huang), ginseng, licorice, hops, and sage.

Hormones

Hormone supplements have received a lot of press lately, as the baby boom refuses to accept the natural aging process and its accompanying health problems. If nature progressively reduces our hormone levels with each passing year, some believe we can enlist the aid of supplements to maintain the hormonal levels and health of a twenty-five year old. But is that really such a good idea? Though some hormones are available without a prescription, it is best to talk to a health care practitioner before implementing hormonal therapies. The topic is included in this book because of the public attention on hormones and because they may present a better alternative to antidepressant drugs. Melatonin and DHEA are two popular hormones being used, at least in part, to relieve depression.

Melatonin is a hormone released from the pineal gland. It is a potent scavenger of "free radicals," the chemical compounds that have been implicated in many diseases, including cancer. Sources of free radicals include: electromagnetic fields (EMF's - from televisions, computer screens, microwaves, x-rays), drugs, alcohol, cigarettes, and other toxic substances. As we age, our bodies produce less melatonin. Lower levels of melatonin interfere with sleep patterns and the bodies ability to fight off damage done by free radicals. If an excessive amount of free radicals is contributing to your depression, melatonin may be of benefit. It is sold without a prescription.

Recommended doses are only 0.1 to 1 mg, two or three times a week, an hour before bedtime.

Melatonin has become extraordinarily popular as a sleep aid. But users should keep in mind that it is an artificially-produced hormone. If anxiety and sleeplessness are causing you to consider melatonin, it may be better to try valerian as a remedy first, because it has no known side effects. Melatonin is reputed to have numerous other medicinal benefits that are detailed in several new books which have dramatically increased the popularity of the hormone. However, I would say that taking hormones would be among the last of my choices -- I would try more natural remedies first.

DHEA (Dehydroepiandrosterone) is a hormone that helps our bodies make estrogen and androgen (and subsequently testosterone). DHEA levels start declining in our twenties, and promoters of DHEA believe that supplements can bring back youthful vigor and libido, restore memory, strengthen the immune system, and improve mood. Those who insist on trying DHEA should start small with only 5 mg daily, though it may be difficult to find supplements in such small doses.

Tracking the Effectiveness of Herbal Supplements

Now that you have some basic information about a few herbal alternatives, you can select some to try one at a time. If you are truly committed to feeling better, you will try at least one TODAY. Take the recommended doses (which are typically printed on the manufacturer's bottle) for at least a week (unless you notice and adverse reaction and should stop), then record the effectiveness in the log in *Exercise 3-1*. Remember that these supplements are much more gentle and subtle than pharmaceutical drugs. You won't likely notice an instant reaction. But over time, your mood should elevate somewhat.

Exercise 3-1

❦ Personal Herbal Supplements Log ❦

Herb/Tonic	Date/Duration	Good Results?
Ginseng		
Ginko Biloba		
St. John's Wort*		
Valerian		
Evening Primrose		
Sage		
Garlic		
Echinacea		
Bee Pollen		

*Do not use St. Johns Wort for extended periods, or with anti-depressant drugs without consulting your health care practitioner.

Herbal Teas

Five thousand years ago, Asian cultures discovered the healing power of tea. Since then, the use of teas has spread globally. Tea is one of the most popular drinks in the world, second only to water. Today, many companies produce teas aimed at providing relief for various ailments. Many herbs can be made into "teas," which are more correctly called "herbal infusions."

You could grow your own herbs and make your own infusions, but for the purposes of this book, we will concentrate of the kinds of infusions that you can find in your health food or grocery store. Many of the teas, or infusions, discussed here are readily available in convenient tea bags.

Teas will be much more effective if you skip the sugar, sugar substitute, and creamers. However, you could sweeten the tea with royal jelly, which is much like honey but with additional energizing properties. Also, make the tea using distilled water, especially if your water supply is tainted.

If circumstances allow, take a moment of repose to enjoy your tea as you drink it. The ceremony of tea making and drinking can be a brief moment of luxury, a simple pleasure in a busy world. Because it is hot, you can't gulp it down. You have to drink it slowly, consciously, and calmly. It is especially enjoyable if you drink from a fine china cup, stirring any cream or sweeteners with a silver spoon. If you don't have a set of china or silver, an enjoyable stroll through a local antique shop to look for odd pieces will surely turn up something suitable for a small cost. (If you use your microwave to heat your water, do not use china but some other appropriate container to heat the water.)

Many of the same herbs used in teas are also used for similar purposes in aromatherapy as you will see in Chapter Four. Others are available as supplements, as stated earlier. You will encounter some of the same names as you read further along.

The following teas or infusions may be helpful in treating your depression. Use whatever is right for you. If your depression has you feeling anxious, you will want to try some sedative, calming herbs. If you are lethargic, you should try some invigorating, stimulating herbs.

Green and Black Teas. True teas must come from the leaves of tea trees. Teas have some caffeine and are stimulating like coffee, but to a lesser degree. Black teas have less caffeine than coffee. Green teas have less caffeine than black teas or coffee, and they help fight toxins in the body that may be contributing to your depression. Green tea is especially reputed to be an immune system builder, inhibiting the activity of viruses. Green tea also helps to fight cancer and to lower cholesterol. Green teas can be a delicious way to improve your health and indirectly relieve depression.

The following infusions are not derived from tea tree leaves and are not true teas. However, we will refer to them as teas for the sake of simplicity.

Chamomile tea has a calming effect, as is one of the most popular tea drinks in the world. It can be used to treat depression and insomnia. It has a pleasant, floral taste with a bitter afternote.

Siberian Ginseng helps you cope with stress, strengthen the immune system, improve mental alertness, and increase energy levels. (See also Chapter Three for taking Siberian Ginseng in tablet form.) Ginseng is becoming such a popular drink that it is often available at gas station-convenience stores.

Lavender used in teas is also known for its calming effects. Its sharp, perfumy taste is too strong to drink without blending with other herbs.

Valerian has a calming effect, but a bitter, disagreeable taste and smell. Well... to be quite honest, it stinks. But it is very effective. It must be blended with other herbs or flavors to be acceptably palatable.

Linden blossom is very popular in Europe, but difficult to find in the United States due to the high harvesting costs reflected in the price. Linden blossom helps lower blood pressure and soothe nervous tension.

Lemon balm has a flowery, soothing lemon flavor that blends well with chamomile. It can be a mild sedative and digestive aid, and can be used daily.

Sage has an intense camphor flavor that is enjoyable when mixed with lemon and honey, but should not be used by pregnant women, nor for extended periods of time.

Rose hips helps to relieve stress and has a high Vitamin C content.

Postpartum tea is for that special kind of depression which commonly occurs in mothers immediately following the birth of a new baby. This depression is understandable given all of the physical and hormonal changes her body has endured. Robin Lim, in her book *After the Baby's Birth ... A Woman's Way to Wellness*, recommends a tea composed of comfrey, false unicorn, licorice root, red raspberry leaves, and shepherd's purse, all in equal parts. She recommends drinking the tea for the first four days following the baby's birth, to help the body to heal and adjust to breast-feeding. You should be able to locate these herbs in your local health store. To save time and energy, you may want to make it by the gallon. While this tea is targeted at your physical health, it may help your mental health simply by helping you feel physically better and give you more energy to bond with your baby. (Note: If you have liver problems, leave the comfrey out of the recipe.)

Prepackaged blends are available for a variety of purposes and ailments. Some of the best and most readily available herbal tea blends are made by Celestial Seasonings®, Alvita (Remeteas™), and Traditional Medicinals®. Their teas are available in tea bag form, and the packaging usually makes the medicinal use of the tea very clear with names like Sleepytime®, Lullaby™, Mellow Magic™, PMS Tea™, and Morning Thunder® (with significant caffeine). Celestial Seasonings' products are available at most grocery stores. Traditional Medicinals and Alvita teas are more easily found in health food stores.

Homeopathy and Floral Essences

Homeopathy and floral essences are relatively newer forms of natural medicine, and are worth some consideration as you identify remedies for depression.

Homeopathy. Homeopathy is a 200 year old science, created by Samuel Hahnemann to cure a host of illnesses including depression. He was dissatisfied with the toxic medicinal treatments of his day, such as mercury, and was looking for a form of medicine that was not injurious to the patient. Homeopathic medicine diagnoses illnesses and treats them with natural substances so diluted that they can cause no harm, and in many cases they act as a remedy.

Hahnemann's new medicine had many celebrity followers in the early years. Almost a century ago it fell into disrepute as the 1910 Flexner Report supported (some would say caused) the move toward modern medicine (surgery and drugs) and away from natural healing medicines such as homeopathy and chiropractic. In recent years, homeopathy has regained much of its respect, at least in the natural medicine field. I have personally used homeopathic remedies for my asthma for two years now. In my case, they have been far superior to any pharmaceutical drugs I have taken, and unlike pharmaceutical drugs, the homeopathic drugs did not produce any negative side effects (like the irregular heartbeats of my pharmaceutical asthma medicine).

Homeopathy has identified several remedies for treating depression. Treatments can be purchased at health food stores and nutrition centers.

- Arum metalicam. Recommended if you are a high achiever, but feel like a failure when you are depressed.

- Arsenicum. Recommended if your depression is accompanied by anxiety and fear of impending poverty or preoccupation with death. And yes, just like it sounds, it is made by diluting arsenic (a poison) to a point where it is harmless.

- Ignatia. Recommended for those suffering from grief, especially the loss of a loved one.

- Sepia. Recommended for exhausted housewives feeling despair, uselessness, and isolation, usually at the "empty-nest" stage of life.

To learn more about homeopathy or to locate a homeopathic practitioner near you, contact:

International Foundation for Homeopathy
PO Box 7
Edmonds, WA 98020
(206) 776-4147

Homeopathic Academy of Naturopathic Physicians
12132 S.E. Foster Place
Portland, OR 97266
(503) 761-3298

National Center for Homeopathy
801 N. Fairfax, Suite 306
Alexandria, VA 22314
(703) 548-7790

Floral Essences. We have all experienced a sense of pleasure from the delightful fragrances of flowers. In the 1930's, an English physician named Edward Bach developed the use of "flower essences" for treatment of health problems, because he was dissatisfied with the results of modern medicine's surgery and drugs. Dr. Bach was inspired by the use of diluted solutions in homeopathy. Flower essences are highly diluted solutions made from water in which flower petals have floated. Typically, a dosage is four drops, either under the tongue or in a glass of water, four times a day. Thirty-eight different kinds of flowers are believed to offer emotional healing. A combination of five flowers is used to make Rescue Remedy®, which is for use in particularly stressful situations.

The essences are used to help bring the user to a state of balance and calmness, so they can more easily deal with the issues at hand. Flower essences are produced by a number of sources, but the most readily available is likely to be Bach™ Flower Essences. In order to identify the correct essence for your situation, you may want to call an essence therapist, who will guide you through a number of personality questions so that your recommended treatment will be tailored for your individual needs. Therapists are available at the following toll free phone numbers:

Nelson Bach, USA (800) 334-0843

Flower Essence Society (800) 548-0075

While there are certainly critics and disbelievers of such treatments, the number of believers is increasing. It doesn't cost much to give it a try if you are willing to be open-minded. The Rescue Remedy®, for example, is available for approximately $15 for 20 ml, or (.7 fl oz) at health food stores.

Tracking the Effectiveness of Herbal Teas, Etc.

Now we will take some time to evaluate the effects of herbal teas, homeopathy, and flower essences have on your mood. This will likely necessitate a trip to the health food store or grocer to buy the products in question. For less than ten dollars you can purchase a supply of two or three teas or tea blends. You may want to bring this book with you as you shop. Upon return, as you complete *Exercise 3-2*, be sure to note whether or not the teas had a calming or energizing effect in the Results column. In the Y/N column, note a "yes" or "no" response for whether or not you should add this element to your personal plan to help ward off depression. Remember that at different times of the day, you will want to use teas with different effects on your system. Be sensitive to any results; the effects are subtle.

Exercise 3-2

Personal Log for Herbal Teas and Floral Essences

Teas	Date/Duration	Good Results?
Green Tea		
Chamomile		
Lavender		
Ginseng		
Valerian		
Linden Blossom		
Lemon Balm		
Sage		
Rose hips		
Other Teas:		
Floral Essences		
Homeopathy		

Chapter Four: Using Essential Oils

"Ointment and perfume delight the heart."
Proverbs 27:9

Essential oils have been used successfully for therapeutic purposes for thousands of years, in addition to their use in fragrant perfumes. Essential oils are made from the hormones of plants and from the concentrated active ingredients of herbs. The most common extraction methods are pressing and distillation. Recently, science has begun to verify anti-viral, anti-bacterial, analgesic, expectorant, anti-depressant, antiseptic, insecticide, stimulant, diuretic, astringent, and other important properties of various essential oils. While science is in the process of verifying the effects, it has not been able to explain them fully. But something in the human physiology responds positively to essential oils, and we can add essential oils to our list of tools available to alleviate depression.

Aromatherapy is the use of essential oils for healing purposes. This chapter will cover the preparation and use of essential oils in aromatherapy. I highly recommend *The Illustrated Encyclopedia of Essential Oils,* by Julia Lawless, for readers who want to learn more about the healing properties of essential oils for a wide variety of ailments. The book is beautifully illustrated and easy to read.

Shopping for Essential Oils

As you shop for essential oils, be sure you are getting the real thing. Read the labels carefully, or you may end up purchasing some kind of synthetic product which will have no curative powers and you will have wasted your money. Make sure the label says "essential oil." A term such as "fragrance oil" on any product can be misleading; it does not mean "essential oil," and you should keep shopping.

Be especially wary when shopping in some of the retail chain stores. Their staffs may not be well-trained and they may assure you that their products are essential oils, but if the label doesn't say "essential oil," don't buy it for aromatherapy purposes. You would be wasting your money.

Essential oils are typically sold in small glass bottles, usually containing about 9-10 ml or about 1/3 of an ounce. Prices are usually less than $10, but some oils will cost more if the extraction process is more costly due to the type of the plant. Lavender is one of the essential oils that seems to command a higher price than the majority of essential oils, but it is one of the best essential oils to have in your possession, because it can be used for a variety of purposes.

Use of Essential Oils

Essential oils are highly concentrated and must be diluted in base oils for massage purposes. They should never be taken internally because they could cause a toxic reaction.

Care of Essential Oils

Essential oils should be stored in dark glass bottles, never plastic. The bottles should be closed tightly because the oils evaporate when exposed to air.

Essential Oils to Treat Depression and Related Problems

The chart in *Figure 4-1* displays the use of some essential oils for depression and other closely related problems of anxiety, fatigue, insomnia, and stress. In each case, the use of oils is appropriate in baths, massage, and vaporization, as will be explained later in this chapter. The names of some of the herbs discussed in Chapter Three also appear in this chapter. This is because many herbal plants used for teas can also be processed into useful essential oils.

Figure 4-1

Essential Oils to Treat Depression and Related Problems

Essential Oil	Depression	Anxiety	Fatigue	Insomnia	Stress
Bergamot	x				x
Chamomile				x	x
Jasmine	x	x	x		x
Lavender	x	x	x	x	x
Lemon Balm		x		x	x
Orange Blossom	x			x	x
Rose*	x				x
Sage*	x		x		
Sandalwood	x				
Valerian				x	x
Ylang Ylang	x	x			

*Rose and sage should not be used during pregnancy.

Massage and Aromatherapy

The most common form of aromatherapy is massage. Massage helps improve circulation which contributes to healing, and also is incredibly pleasurable, increasing our ability to relax.

In aromatherapy massage, a few drops of appropriate essential oils are added to the base massage oil. The ratio of essential oil to base oil calls for a dilution of one to three percent. The more common base massage oils are made from nuts or seeds. You may want to chose your base oil from among the following:

* *Walnut oil* - balances the nervous system
* *Wheatgerm oil* - an anti-oxidant
* *Evening Primrose oil* - for cell regeneration and healing
* *Olive oil* - vitamin-rich, keeps skin supple

Other possible base oils are almond, apricot kernel, grapeseed, and peanut. After you have chosen your base oil, you then choose the appropriate essential oil. Essential oils should be used in a one to three percent proportion to the base oil. For each massage, pour a little more than a teaspoon into a saucer or bowl and add two or three drops of essential oil. A skilled aromatherapist can provide effective combinations of effective oils, but there is enough information here to get you started.

If you were to prepare a bulk amount of massage oil for future use, an ounce of base oil would be accompanied by 7 to 25 drops of essential oil.

Massage is also healing for another reason: the documented but unexplained healing powers of human touch. Bear in mind that we are not talking about sexual massage here, we are talking about therapeutic massage. As I see it, we have three basic choices when it comes to massage: 1) pay a professional, 2) hope your significant other will treat you, and 3) do-it-yourself.

Professional massage - Professional massage therapists are generally hired for half hour or hour time periods. Find your therapist by getting referrals from friends or by checking the yellow pages under Massage or Beauty Salons, some of which have begun to offer aromatherapy massage and facials. Health clubs and health spas typically have associations with professional massage therapists. When you make the appointment, make sure the therapist will be using the kind of oils you need or is agreeable to using the massage oils that you bring with you to the appointment.

Partner massage. If you have a spouse or significant other, it probably won't be hard to get a massage if you offer one in return. This method has several advantages. It costs nothing more than the cost of massage oils. It helps you relax together, getting you more "in sync" with one another. It can help improve your relationship and your communication, and each partner appreciates being on the receiving end of such personal, undivided attention and pleasure. It can also be a way to ease any tension between you if you've just had an argument. Making up is always good for your mood.

For single parents, don't overlook the obvious partner -- your child. Exchange foot massages after a long hard day at work and school. You'll both feel better, and it can be a chance to catch up on the events of the day. When I was a child I suffered from severe bouts of asthma. But I felt immense relief when my mother would massage my feet. I now realize that her loving touch had tremendous healing ability.

Self-massage. Well, if there is no one around to massage you, and you can't afford to see a professional massage therapist, you can still massage your face, scalp, arms, legs and feet. Unfortunately, this method doesn't have nearly the same relaxation impact as having someone else do the work, but it can still be beneficial. Just put on some very relaxing music, settle into a comfortable chair, light some scented candles, and chose your favorite massage oils. You will feel much more centered and relaxed than if you hadn't gone through this ritual.

> As you experience the pleasure of using essential oils in aromatherapy, you may decide to try other oils for other purposes. Please note that the following oils should not be used during pregnancy or breast-feeding: Bay, Basil, Clary Sage, Comfrey, Fennel, Hyssop, Juniper, Marjoram, Melissa, Myrrh, Rose, Rosemary, Sage, and Thyme.

Other Aromatherapy Methods

Essential oils are also effective when they gently enter the body through the action of breathing in the vaporized fragrances. There are many mechanisms for this method of aromatherapy.

Figure 4-2

Other Ways to Use Essential Oils in Aromatherapy

Bath	Add 8 to 10 drops to your bathwater. Some of the aroma will rise with steam, if the water is hot enough. Some will also be absorbed by your skin. A doubly-effective form of aromatherapy.
Humidifiers	Add a few drops of oil to the water in your humidifier. At nighttime, lavender is an excellent choice.
Room sprays	A few drops of essential oil in an atomizer filled with water can be used to fill the air in your home or office with healing fragrances.
Light bulbs	A drop of oil on the top of a table lamp's lightbulb will be diffused into the air from the heat of the bulb. Rings are also manufactured to fit atop light bulbs and to hold essential oils. The rings are probably safer and are less messy.
Candles	Carefully add a drop to the hot wax of a lit candle, or buy special aromatherapy candles.
Handkerchiefs or Tissues	A drop or two of an essential oil on a handkerchief can be kept on hand and brought out whenever you like. In earlier times, ladies put lavender in their handkerchiefs to help cover the smell of horses or other disagreeable smells of the streets.

Suppliers of Essential Oils

I am including a brief list of some suppliers of essential oils for my readers who may be home-bound or for some other reason, do not have easy access to local retailers who provide essential oils.

Aroma Land
Rt. 20, Box 29AL
Santa Fe, NM 87505
(800) 933-5267
Fax (505) 438-7223

Health Center for Better Living
1414 Rosemary Lane
Naples, FL 33940-4283
(800) 544-4225

The Joint Adventure
PO Box 824
Rogers, AZ 72757
(800) 898-PURE
(501) 636-3785 Fax

Recording Your Response to Aromatherapy

As you try a variety of essential oils, record the effects you notice in the following log. Knowing what works for you will help you design your personal maintenance and rescue plans in Chapter Ten.

Exercise 4-1

❦ Personal Log for Essential Oils ❦

Essential Oil Tried	Helps me to Relax?	Gives me energy?
Bergamot		
Chamomile		
Jasmine		
Lavender		
Lemon Balm		
Orange Blossom		
Rose		
Sage		
Sandalwood		
Valerian		
Ylang Ylang		
Other:		

Chapter Five: Using Nature's Healing Forces

"There can be no very black melancholy to him who lives in the midst of Nature, and has his senses still."

Henry David Thoreau from *Walden*

Who among us doesn't feel a little more at peace, in touch with a deeper part of ourselves, when we are outdoors amidst the trees, grass, flowers, hillsides, canyons, and shorelines? There is something about nature that calms the soul, clears the mind, and heals the body. Some believe that nature actually transfers energy to the human beings in its midst. Maybe it does, with a kind of natural magic. Nature can provide comfort, grounding, and serenity when we may be feeling lost, disconnected, or depressed. When we are surrounded by nature and are a good distance from, or at least out of sight of, "civilization" we are probably breathing the cleanest air that our body has known since our last such encounter with the earth itself.

Our bodies can't help but be cleansed and renewed by the fresh-as-it-gets oxygen from the trees and by the reduction in airborne toxins that exist in our daily lives. In our modern society, our bodies are constantly bombarded by the vehicle exhaust fumes, germ-ridden air of "sick" office buildings, industrial air and water pollution, pesticides on our food, radiation waves from our computer screens and even carpet glue fumes. Is it any wonder that we sometimes feel insufficiently armed to do battle with feelings of depression? We have wasted a lot of physical defensive ammunition just to survive!

Nature Visit

A visit with nature can be an uplifting experience. It's also an ideal time to be alone with yourself and hear yourself think. If you live in a very urban setting and have few transportation options, take a walk to a local city park. It's not the best option, but it's better than sitting inside your apartment. If you live in the suburbs and have a car, pull out a map of your area and plan a trip to a nearby state park or beach. For safety's sake, stay within view of other people but far enough away to have some privacy. If you are among the fortunate who have an abundance of trees right outside your front or back door, you may not have to travel at all, unless you want a change of scenery.

You may want to plan two types of trips. One that you could make on an almost daily basis (a natural spot close to home or work), and one where nature is on a grander scale but its inconvenient location means that your visits will be less frequent.

Remember that the point of your trip is to make you feel better, and to have the effects last as long as possible. Therefore, these guidelines should help make the trip more enjoyable and effective:

1. Listen to the sounds of nature and your own thoughts. Don't bring a radio. After a few hours of listening to yourself, you may have more insight into the root causes of your depression. That insight is very valuable.

2. If you must bring something to read, even if only as a prop to discourage inquisitive strangers, make sure it is inspirational reading, not the latest murder mystery.

3. Dress in layers so you can be comfortable regardless of the weather.

4. Bring some outdoor essential like sunscreen, natural non-toxic bug spray, sunglasses, a hat, blanket, nutritious food (you'll be there a couple of hours and you might get hungry), and water or juice (no alcohol). You may also want to bring tissues or a handkerchief. Let's face it -- when we get in touch with ourselves, we sometimes need a good cry.

5. Go alone, or if you must go with someone, make sure it is a friend who can be quiet for long stretches of time and won't spend time talking about their problems. You have a right to be selfish about this.

6. Bring a journal to write down any thoughts you have and want to remember or decisions you make about actions you will take.

7. Keep an open mind. Don't brood on the bad things, but consider what you may have learned from them. Think about the things in your life that you appreciate and are grateful for.

8. Give thanks to God, or whatever you believe in, for your blessings and ask for help in dealing with your life's difficulties. Turning over your problems to a higher authority will help you feel that a burden has been lifted.

9. Breathe rhythmically and deeply for ten consecutive inhale/exhale cycles. This helps to flush out the toxins in your respiratory system. Notice how much calmer you feel afterwards.

10. Leave the earth as you found it. Properly dispose of your trash.

When we are surrounded by nature, life seems more in balance. We gain a refreshed perspective on life and its problems. We see that nature is constantly healing and renewing itself. We start to realize that we are part of one big ecosystem. We may be the center of our own world, but we are not the center of the whole world. Sitting on a beach, the waves roll in just like they have for millions of years. From that perspective, it is important to remember that it is not our lives that are insignificant, but our problems.

"That's great for other people," you say "but I am a single parent. Who's going to watch the kids while I run off to the beach?" Well, in cases like that, where you are a caregiver with little chance of getting away from your responsibilities, you must improvise. Bring the kids with you, but try to invite someone along that may be able to keep an eye on them for a short time, at least, so that you can have some "alone" time. If that's not possible, the trip, even with kids in tow, will probably still be very beneficial for you. Give it a try.

While you are there, be sure to take a few minutes for some deep-breathing. Focus your thoughts on your breath, slowly inhale deeply, hold your breath for a second or two, then exhale slowly until you have emptied your lungs. Do that ten times, remaining focused on the breathing process. You will find yourself more relaxed, and you will have eliminated many toxins in your body with those deep exhales. This is a good exercise to do every day, in fact.

Some readers may be homebound and still want to experience nature. In those cases, it may be useful to purchase videos or audiotapes of nature sights and sounds.

Special Vacation Trips to Visit Nature

Sometimes, an afternoon at the beach is not enough to restore your energy levels or elevate your mood. Several days interacting with nature may be called for. Be sure and take some vacation time in a natural, scenic, tranquil environment.

My husband and I recently made a trip to the Grand Canyon, and it was as awesome as we had believed it would be. Not only did it make us ponder God, wind, water, earth, and time, but it provided us with mental images that will never leave us. I can easily imagine a time of stress when I will be able to close my eyes and see the grandeur of the canyon -- and feel at peace again. Sometimes, the visions we create on vacation can serve us many years in the future. Keep that in mind as you plan your vacations.

Meditation Gardens

Some cities have public gardens that are very conducive to thoughtful meditation. Some cover vast acres, others are quite small. Seek out nearby gardens that you can visit on a regular basis, or that you can use for inspiration in constructing your own meditation garden at home. You may want to sketch out some ideas for your own garden while you are there, to help reinforce any gardening plans you may have.

Bringing Nature Indoors

You can also bring nature home by planting indoor gardens. Working with the earth's soil is very therapeutic. If you have a patio or balcony, plant a container garden. Learn to decorate with plants indoors and enhance the ambiance of your home, while providing a source of indoor fresh oxygen. Put taller plants in the back and smaller ones in the front for a good display. Create your own area of retreat with comfortable chairs or benches surrounded by greenery and colorful flowers. Then you can spend time every day in your own oasis, perhaps with a cup of healing tea.

Consider the flowers and herbs discussed in other chapters of this book when planning what to grow in your garden. Consider planting lavender, sage, and chamomile, for instance. You may be able to use them in your cooking or to make herbal teas. An herbal garden can help reinforce your commitment to use healing herbs.

Also, keep fresh-cut flowers on your desk or in the room where you spend much of your time. The wonderful scent of fresh flowers can't help but make you feel better.

Keeping green plants in your office area is also a good idea. Good air filtering systems are not a high priority for most employers, and you should try to counter the effects of any bad air that is being circulated in your building. Plants provide us with fresh oxygen.

Gemstones and Crystals

For thousands of years, cultures around the world have attributed healing properties to gemstones. Even today, many people believe that stones have "energy fields" or "healing vibrations." No New Age fair is complete without at least one booth for crystals and gemstones. Some stones associated with healing depression include: orange calcite (for post-partum depression), chrysoprase (for feelings of inferiority), jade (for confidence and wisdom while you assess problems), lapis lazuli (for serenity and self-acceptance), moonstone (for dealing with the changing structures of life and for some women's health issues), mordenite (to break free from negativity), seamanite (to bring a sense of hope), peridot (when grieving the loss of love), smoky quartz, ruby (for protection against unhappiness), sapphire (to eliminate unwanted thoughts), and topaz (to replace negativity with joy).

Even those who do not attribute mystical powers to stones and crystals, can't help but be taken with their beauty and perhaps be a little entranced with their mysterious markings and designs. Polished stones have a tactile allure; they feel good to touch.

For the true believers, there is a kind of science associated with the use of stones. To rid them of the vibrations of previous handlers, for instance, American Indians cleansed the stones in salt water or running streams. It is considered a general rule not to lend or borrow gemstones. Larger crystals are believed to be more effective than smaller ones. One of the most common ways to use crystals is to wear them as a necklace pendant. Some people also wear Native American decorative leather, crystal-filled medicine pouches around their necks. You may want to keep a small bowl of crystals and stones on your desk for inspiration.

While science pooh-poohs the idea of energizing gemstones, I don't think the idea should be completely discounted. Just because science has not been able to prove the existence of something does not mean it doesn't exist; it may just mean that it is not within the realm of our comprehension or technology. There is no "love-o-scope" to predict when love will happen, or a "love-o-meter" to measure love when it exists. But no one can deny that love is a very real and powerful force in this world. Maybe there are other things just as real and powerful, and just as unmeasurable. Just maybe. Do you have an open mind?

While writing this book, I tried using the power of stones for the first time. When I hit a moment of "writer's block," I spent some time with stones said to aid in communication. For whatever reason (wishful thinking, luck, coincidence, or "stone-power"), the stones had me back on the writing track within a half-hour each time I used them. With success like that, I suspect I will try to use them again in the future.

Working Outdoors

We can't all be forest rangers, but we can try to bring as much of our work outside as possible. If you have a professional job that requires a lot of unpaid overtime, why not leave the office and read those reports in the outdoors? Make those calls with a portable phone from your lounge chair in the back yard. Jot down that memo under a shade tree. You may find that the quality of your work improves and your thoughts become more creative. And your family will appreciate having you around more often, even if you have to work.

Exercises for Healing with Nature

In *Exercise 5-1*, plan how you can use nature to help heal your depression. In *Exercise 5-2*, after you have carried out your plans, record the results of your actions. Nature must be incorporated into your lifestyle on a regular basis. These exercises are to help you figure out how to do that most effectively. Remember that this is not a one-time effort with instantaneous results. Relief from depression will be gradual and subtle. Nature can help you heal if you call on it with a sense of appreciation and spiritualism.

Exercise 5-1

❦ Strategies for Using Nature's Healing Powers ❦

Less than an hour away, I could visit the following places to get energy from nature:

When I have time to make a longer journey, I should visit:

In order to connect with nature on a daily basis I can:

I am willing to try healing with the following gemstones and crystals:

Exercise 5-2

❦ Results from Using Nature to Heal ❦

My visit to a local nature site resulted in:
(Name the site.)

My visit to a distant nature site resulted in:
(Name the site.)

My use of healing crystals and gemstones resulted in:
(Name the stones.)

Chapter Six: Being Physically Active

One of the most important keys to good physical and mental health, is physical activity. I hesitate to say "exercise" because of the negative associations that many people make with the word. Physical activity helps keep our bodies in proper working order, helps burn unneeded calories, helps ward off chronic illness, and increases our flexibility and strength.

Physical activity also has several important effects on our mental health, all of which are related. We'll discuss them briefly.

First, *physical activity gives us a feeling of control over our bodies.* Knowing that we are gaining physical strength feels powerfully positive, and adds bounce to our step. People suffering from depression often feel completely out of control of their lives and current situations. Having total control of just one thing, our body's physical activities, is one partial remedy for depression. Building physical strength helps to build mental and emotional strength. It makes us feel more powerful.

Physical activity can change the way we walk and how we carry ourselves. Think about how depressed people walk. Slouched, downward-looking, slow, dejected. How do happy, people walk? Quick-paced, energetic, straight-backed, confident. Those latter characteristics are most often found with people who are also in good physical shape. Coincidence? I think not. How do you walk? How do you sit? What message about your mood do you convey to others?

Second, *physical activity releases substances that are good for the brain.* Exercise (especially vigorous exercise) releases neurochemicals called catecholamines, which depressed patients often have in lower than normal levels. The "runner's high" is caused by the body's release of endorphins (after aerobic exercise), which are natural antidepressants. I recommend some moments of solitude after exercise, preferably in a natural setting such as under a tree, to fully experience the "natural high" that exercise provides.

Depressed patients are often prescribed anti-depressant drugs, but if the depression is the result of a shortage of these chemicals, isn't natural production through exercise a far more superior solution to the problem? In *Manifesto for a New Medicine*, Dr. James Gordon states that his experience has led him to believe that the single best therapy for moderate cases of depression and anxiety is physical exercise.

Third, *physical activity helps relieve stress and anxiety*, perhaps by adding another dimension or interest to our lives and by providing more balance. For example, if you are doing well in a neighborhood tennis tournament, a bad day at work won't send you into a tailspin because work is no longer the only thing going on in your life. You have an identity outside of your job. Also, exercise is a great opportunity to meet new friends, or visit with old ones. For instance, you can join a volleyball team or get a jogging partner.

Fourth, *physical activity creates energy*. Many people who feel listless, feel that way because of a lack of physical motion. Inertia begets inertia. But, after a little exercise, most people feel more rejuvenated and energized. If you are feeling listless and tired now, don't wait for the energy to exercise because it may not come. At first, you may have to operate on sheer willpower. But shortly, you will find that you have the necessary energy to maintain a regimen, and you will find it very enjoyable.

Fifth, *physical activity helps ward off illness* (especially chronic diseases), which can often lead to depression. This fact is supported by scientific studies, and is true for people of all ages.

Scientific studies have shown that a lack of exercise can lead to depression. It follows, then, that physical activity must be a planned, key part of your lifestyle in your battle against depression.

In order for your plan to be successful, it must be easily sustainable. In other words, it should not be too inconvenient, like joining a health club on the other side of town. If you have home exercise equipment, set it up in front of a television, so that you can pass the time quickly and painlessly. Exercise during your favorite show so that you will develop positive associations with the thought of exercising.

A successful program should also be based upon activities that you enjoy, with a schedule that you can keep. Activities you enjoyed in your youth may be the kinds of things that would still hold your interest today. If you kind find a partner to help you stay on schedule, all the better. Signing up for team sports at the local YWCA or YMCA may also be a great solution, and can also be a great place to meet new people and help you get out of the rut that you may be in.

Your physical activity can be in any form, whether a sport or an exercise regimen. It could even be reacquainting yourself with an activity that you used to participate in when you were younger. Here is a list of possibilities, including some hobbies that provide some physical benefits. Try at least one.

Aerobics
Ballet
Baseball
Basketball
Biking (including stationary)
Canoeing
Carpentry
Cross-country skiing
Dance
Floor exercises (sit-ups, push-ups, etc.)
HealthRider (or similar machines)

Housecleaning
Gardening
Gymnastics
Hiking
Karate
Jogging
Judo
Lacrosse
NordicTrack (or similar machines)
Racquetball
Rowing
Rugby
Running
Skating (Ice and In-line)
Skiing
Softball
Stair climbing
Step Aerobics
Stretching
Swimming
Table tennis (Ping Pong)
Tai Chi
Tennis
Volleyball
Walking
Water skiing
Weightlifting
Wood-chopping
Yoga

When making a decision on which activities to pursue, consideration should be given to your general level of health, and to the costs of equipping yourself for a new sport. You may want to start gradually, and build up to higher levels of activity. Walking is probably the cheapest and best sport for beginners. Talk to a health care practitioner before doing anything too strenuous.

Physical activity is a great way to spend time with your kids, friends, and significant other. Be sure to include them in your plans if possible. You could all sign up for a class together. If attending regular classes is not a viable option, you may be able to find a video on your area of interest. Then you can exercise when it is convenient for you. There are several videos available on Yoga, Tai Chi, and aerobics. (Living Arts company distributes a *YogaKids* video. Call (800) 254-8464.)

One of the most encouraging findings in recent research is that the cumulative effect of every physical movement that you make is beneficial to your health. Physical activity includes a lot of the typical activities of daily living such as walking from place to place, vacuuming, and mowing the lawn. If you are unable to commit to a regular exercise routine, then decide how you can accumulate more physical activity in every day. Take the stairs, at least for a few flights. Park farther away from your destination, so that you have further to walk. Walk around the office to visit a co-worker, rather than use e-mail. Bicycle with your children.

Exercise 6-1 gives you an opportunity to think about how you can incorporate more exercise into your life on a regular basis. Be sure and follow up with the real exercise. In fact, when you finish this chapter, get up and DO SOMETHING. Remember, ANY physical activity is better than none. Get up and get going, even if it is just to walk around the block. Take that first step.

Exercise 6-1

Becoming More Active

My favorite sports as a child were:

Sports/activities that I should pursue more are:

I can work exercise into my daily routine by:

Friends/family who could participate with me include:

Equipment I need to obtain include:

After searching the yellow pages and comparing prices, hours, and amenities, I will join the following gym/YMCA/YWCA:

Its amenities include:

Its phone number is:

Its hours are:

Chapter Seven: Creating a Positive Environment

Many aspects of our environment can positively or negatively influence our moods. An environment can excite, calm, or provoke anxiety. It is extremely important to manage our environment and design surroundings that will promote positive thoughts, such as feelings of comfort, love, and happiness.

The Use of Color

Colors affect our emotions and our physiology, whether we realize it or not. So it makes sense that we can learn more about how to use color to our advantage to affect moods.

There is a field of study called Chromotherapy, which uses color in the treatment of disease and in maintaining high levels of wellness. You have surely seen colors of flowers that gave you a sense of happiness and delight, and been in rooms where the use of color made you feel better just to be there.

We will not delve deeply into chromotherapy in this book. We will only cover some of the basics ways colors affect our physiology. Readers are encouraged to do their own research. *Nurturing Happiness* is only intended to be a starting point in your quest for information and ideas.

Figure 7-1

Colors and Their Physiological Impact

Red

Sight of the color produces adrenaline in the body to be released. Elevates blood pressure. Increases rate of breathing. Heightens sensitivity of taste buds. Heightens sense of smell.

Yellow

While the color has appeal to many people because it seems so bright and cheerful, you may be surprised to hear that yellow stimulates feelings of caution, adds to stress, and can trigger allergies.

Blue

The most tranquilizing color of all is a strong sky-blue. Blue slows the heart rate, deepens breathing, reduces perspiration, and lowers body temperature. It also eliminates the fight or flight response and reduces appetite.

Brown

This earth tone allows the metabolism to function properly. It also: helps dispel mental depression, promotes the production of serotonin (a neuro-transmitter), and reduces irritability. Additionally, it reduces fatigue (and perhaps chronic fatigue syndrome), and increases the production of the amino acid tryptophan (which affects moods, sleep, immunity, and migraine headaches).

Violet

Stimulates the upper brain and depresses the lymphatics, heart muscle, and motor nerves. It helps control irritability, reduces hunger, and helps calm some cases of mental illness.

Green

May help people with hay fever alergies by elevating blood histamine levels. Produces favorable metabolic responses. Helps improve eyesight or ease tired eyes. Helps allergic reactions to foods.

Orange

Appeals only to a limited number of people. Slows the heart rate, and increases appetite. When combined with blue, it can provide a sense of security and calmness.

❦❦❦

These characterizations of responses to colors are generalizations, and you may not have the same reactions. The point remains, that you should learn to become aware of your response to various colors, and try to surround yourself with colors that make you feel better.

Color surrounds us constantly. What colors are surrounding you now? The colors of walls and draperies? Rugs? Chairs? Sofas? Floor tiles? Desks? Cabinets? Clothes? We can't escape being surrounded by color, since all material things have color.

How can you change the color of your surroundings without spending a fortune? A can of paint and a paintbrush can result in some of the least expensive and most effective redecorating. You could also add plants or flower arrangements to your home or office. Artwork, such as posters and paintings, can bring needed colors to a room. Slipcovers for chairs and sofas can also be a relatively inexpensive way to change your color scheme. Ponder some potential changes for a few minutes and you will surely think of some suitable ideas worth trying. *Exercise 7-1* will help give you some ideas to integrate color therapy into your plans for elevating your moods.

Exercise 7-1

Personal Plan for Color Therapy

The colors that make me happiest are:

I should surround myself with the following colors:

I can change the color of my home by:

I can change the color of my work environment by:

I can change the color of by wardrobe by:

Other color therapy ideas:

Healing Sights and Sounds

You may not be aware of the effect that the sounds in your environment are having on your mood. Negative thoughts may be bombarding your brain from the radio, television, stereo, and walkman. News of atrocious crimes can burden our spirit. Songs of hatred and violence in most rap music, are detrimental to our psyche.

Stop and think about the kinds of positive messages you want to hear on a consistent basis, and then adjust your media and music exposure accordingly. This may mean that you watch the news less often. The nightly news may be more upsetting to you than you realize -- especially if you watch it before going to bed. It may also mean that you forgo your favorite TV dramas and switch to comedies instead. Or that your movie/video choices move from mainstream, violence-oriented material to those that are more inspiring, funny, or informative. What you see has a great effect on how you feel. If you want to feel good, watch something with a positive message. It's that simple.

Music has an amazing ability to instantly transform our moods. One song can make us want to dance, and the next can make us want to cry. But isn't that great? Knowing that, we can use music to help manage our moods. We can listen to music that fills our emotional needs and guides us to a happier state. And we can also learn to react to music that negatively influences our moods by immediately turning it off.

When making music choices, think about how you feel compared to how you want to feel. Are you stressed and in need of calm? Are you insecure and in need of strength? Are you feeling tired and in need of energy? No matter what you need, there is music for you. Choose the music you need.

Jimmy Buffett's music is great for teaching us not to take ourselves too seriously, and to keep things in perspective. What member of the rat race hasn't dreamed of taking it easy on the beaches of "Margaritaville?"

We can find inspiration in religious music, like gospel, and in pop music. Many top performers have recorded songs about surviving tough times, like Gloria Estefan's song about "coming out of the dark," and Billy Joel's about getting his "second wind." Helen Reddy's anthem "I am Woman" can still make us want to roar, and Gloria Gaynor's pledge of "I will survive!" leaves no doubt about that. You can probably name numerous others. Collect your favorites, and make a tape of the songs that you need to hear most often.

If you are looking for soothing, mystical music, I can't say enough good things about the work of the artist Enja. She has produced some remarkable, haunting, New-Age-yet-ancient-Celtic recordings. An excellent addition to your music collection.

Another source of peaceful, soothing melodies is the Gregorian chant music of the Benedictine Monks of Santo Domingo de Silos. If you are looking to bring calm to your life, there may be no better music. My personal favorite is their first album, "Chant," which hit the music charts in a surprisingly big way. My husband and I often fall asleep to the soft and reassuring sounds of the Monks, and somehow feel a little safer, more protected, and closer to God. Use the next exercise to help you focus on music therapy for relieving depression.

Exercise 7-2

❦ Personal Plan for Music Therapy ❦

Music that gives me energy includes:

Music that brings me peace includes:

Music that gives me inspiration includes:

I can bring more uplifting music into my life by:

The Sounds of Silence

When your senses are bombarded by civilization, it is hard to hear your soul as it speaks to you. Be sure to schedule some time for silence. Unplug the phone, turn off the television and the radio, and enjoy the pleasure of your own company in a quiet environment. Listen to your inner voice as it converses with itself, and works out problems. Hear yourself think. Get reacquainted with yourself.

Feng Shui - The Chinese Art of Placement

Feng Shui (pronounced "fung schway") is an ancient art that is regaining popularity. Its purpose is to maximize the energy "chi" that an environment, such as a home or office, provides to its owner. Some people who have had their home redesigned by a fung schui professional and immediatly sensed an increased energy level. If there are rooms that make you feel stressed or drained of energy, you may want to try learning more about Feng Shui.

Organizing Your Home or Office

When you consider the draining effect that a messy home or office can have on your psyche, it is easy to understand that we should make an effort to keep our homes and offices organized. Take a few minutes each day to organize your surroundings.

Make sure that "everything has a place." You can be more effective and efficient with your time if you don't continually lose track of items that you need. And if you have decorated your environment with personal mementos that keep you looking backward instead of forward in your life, then maybe it is time to clean house, toss out some junk and the emotional baggage that goes with it, and create an organized environment that encourages a bright future.

Exercise 7-3 serves to prompt you into thinking about ways to organize your home or office. You will likely think of many more ways, and you should jot them down and develop a plan to help you get your office and home under control.

Exercise 7-3

Personal Organizational Plan

I can organize my office by getting rid of:

I can organize my office by creating files for:

I can organize my home by getting rid of:

I can organize my home by creating files for:

I can organize my closets by:

I will tackle my organizing efforts in the following order:

Other Considerations

Before moving on to the next chapter, stop to think if there are other aspects of you environment that could be more uplifting. Make note of any other environmental factors that need to be changed.

Chapter Eight: Nurturing Positive Thoughts

"...we must struggle ... and do our best to gain health of mind..."

Plato, *Five Great Dialogues*

Depression fills our minds with negative thoughts, but we can actively promote and nurture the kinds of positive thoughts that give us inspiration, hope, comfort, and joy. We can *train our brain* to take on a more positive outlook on life.

Inspirational Reading

The uplifting effects of reading inspirational reading would be hard to overestimate. Words can provide us with comfort and solace. They can also provide us with a better understanding of life's difficulties and philosophies to help you cope. They can change our way of thinking and provide us with a renewed passion for life.

In the category of inspirational reading, I include not only religious material (such as The Bible, or other religious texts), but also "self-help" books. The best seller lists are full of books that help us delve into the meaning of our lives and how we can improve the quality of our lives. Thought-provoking reading can often reveal to us more about the root causes of our own depression, and provide renewed hope for better days ahead.

The timeless philosophies found in the writing of the Greeks and Romans can still be useful today. If you never studied philosophy in school, you need not be intimidated at the thought. It can be very enjoyable reading, and it is surprising to see how little human nature has changed in the last couple of thousand years. Try:

On Man in the Universe, Aristotle
Meditations, Marcus Aurelius

At the top of my self-help list, is M. Scott Peck's *The Road Less Traveled*. It is a contemporary classic, having been a best seller for several years now. It has helped countless people deal with life's difficulties, and enjoy its gifts.

Sometimes depression seems to be the result of not having gotten what we think we want out of life. If you need some positive messages about aggressively pursuing your goals and dreams, I highly recommend *Awaken the Giant Within*, by Anthony Robbins. This book is so outstanding, it's one of my favorites to give as a gift. Mr. Robbins gives his readers every tool they need to achieve any goal they may have. It is up to the reader to figure out what they truly want out of life, but the book has exercises that help readers figure that out, too.

For many people, loneliness is a factor in their depression. Their friendships and love relationships have not been satisfactory, and may have been so painful that they have lost the desire to try again. If that sounds like you, try reading:

How to Win Friends and Influence People, Dale Carnegie
Dare to Connect, Susan Jeffers, Ph.D.
Are you the One for Me?, Barbara DeAngelis, Ph.D.

If your depression was brought on by the loss of a loved one, (through death, divorce, etc.) try getting inspiration, understanding, and the ability to cope with help from:

Necessary Losses, Judith Viorst
When Bad Things Happen to Good People, Harold Kushner

These books listed are just a few examples. A good library or bookstore will have a wide selection. Check the sections on self-help, religion, philosophy, psychology, or anything else that seems appropriate. *Exercise 8-1* will help you get started in the area of inspirational reading. Be sure and follow through by obtaining the necessary reading material.

Exercise 8-1

❦ Personal Plan for Inspirational Reading ❦

I should seek out inspirational reading on the following topics:

My home library of inspirational reading includes:

I have identified passages in the following books that are especially inspiring:

I will devote the following block of time to inspirational reading on a regular basis:

Smile-in-the-Box

The idea for a "smile-in-the-box" comes from the fact that I love photographs. Looking through photo albums filled with memories of friends and loved ones has always been a source of pleasure for me. Expanding on that idea, it is possible to create a treasure trove of meaningful souvenirs, letters, audio tapes and other mementos that make you smile and laugh, or feel loved, accomplished, or otherwise reminded of happy moments. By physically putting those items in one place, you have an instant source of happiness when life gets you down.

Some things can hardly fail to make you smile or laugh. Consider the *Seinfeld* television show, *Dilbert* books and cartoons, and the antics of baby animals. Make a list of things that make you laugh and figure out a way to incorporate them into your Smile-in-the-Box.

Make or buy an attractive box to contain your "smiles." Then fill it with an assortment of things that inspire you, help you keep your perspective, and fill you with feelings of love and happiness. Consider including letters, greeting cards, articles, books, videos, photos, awards, essential oils... the list is endless, and the contents of your box will be unlike anyone else's. This is a great project for Moms whose children are aware of her depression and want to help, or for teens who are suffering themselves.

Exercise 8-2

❦ Creating a "Smile-in-the-Box" ❦

My list of items to be included in my Smile-in-the-Box includes:

Finding Beauty

Taking time to find the beauty in life is a good way to improve your mental attitude. Visiting an art museum is one of the most inspiring activities around. Seeing the genius of the painters and sculptors from centuries ago can make you in awe of mankind's talent and potential. Most art museums themselves are works of art, especially in our older cities. Their foyers of marble staircases and crystal chandeliers can be like something out of a dream. Theaters, too, can provide inspiration for audiences of classical music, plays, dance, or musicals. Many events may be free of charge, or cost only a token amount. Add some culture to your life and see the happiness it can bring you. This is another activity that is great for including young children. Theatre events often have matinee performances which cost less than the evening shows, offering an opportunity for a real bargain.

Setting Goals

Time after time, studies have shown that people who have a written list of goals are far more likely to achieve their goals and be more successful than those who do not commit their goals to paper. The act of writing down our goals forces us to focus on specifics, and helps define exactly what we want our future to hold. Periodic review and revision of our goals helps us to stay on track and committed to the level of effort required to help us attain our goals.

If you feel at times like your life has no direction, then you probably have not yet defined any goals for yourself. Once you identify your goals, you can then determine the appropriate long term strategies to help you reach those goals. In the short run, you can determine the immediate tasks that embody the long term strategies and help move you along the road to your dreams.

Let's look at an example. Say that one of your lifetime goals is to write a screenplay for what becomes a blockbuster movie. The strategies and tasks might break down like this:

Lifetime Goal:	To write a screenplay for a movie that achieves #1 box office status and pays me $2 million.
Long-term Strategies:	Write the screenplay. Make industry contacts. Consider independent film producers. Aggressively market the screenplay.
Short-term Tasks:	Buy computer and printer. Develop story outline. Join writer's group/attend meetings. Study screenplay writing. Write one scene per week. Create workspace area.

Take some time now and sketch out your lifetime goals, and the steps needed to get you there. Each goal will require its own list of strategies and tasks, but you may find that your strategies for one goal help reinforce your progress toward another goal.

Exercise 8-3

Developing Goals

Lifetime Goals:

Long-term Strategies:

Short-term Tasks:

Visualization

Visualization is the art of picturing your desires in your mind's eye, as if you have already attained them. See yourself sitting in the chair in the office of your ideal job, winning an important negotiation, jogging down the beach in perfect health, writing generous checks to your favorite charities, driving behind the wheel of your dream car, or relaxing at the lake cottage with your ideal mate. Creating powerful images for your future help propel you toward the future you desire. Take a few minutes with *Exercise 8-4* to visualize your version of happiness.

Exercise 8-4

❦ Visualizing Happiness ❦

In *Exercise 1-3*, you developed your personal definition of happiness. Look back at that exercise, and visualize yourself in the happy state that you described. Modify your definition if necessary and repeat this exercise often.

Manifestation Bowl™

Trusting my intuition, I recently made a trip to Sedona, Arizona because I believed it would provide me with the final spurt of energy and inspiration that I needed to finish this book. (I was right.) Sedona is reputed to have extremely high energy fields and is a haven for New Age followers. While there, I purchased a Manifestation Bowl™ from a local New Age store. I had seen them for sale at several stores in Sedona. It has the vague shape of a person whose lap forms the bowl. I liked the concept of the bowl so much that I want to share it with you now. The idea behind the bowl is to write down your goal or wish on a small piece of paper, and place it in the bowl, perhaps along with a small crystal. Then visualize the goal coming true. The ritual of the manifestation bowl, explained further in its accompanying directions, is helpful in turning your dreams into reality. The bowls, which cost less than twenty dollars, are manufactured and trademarked by Art and Soul, P.O. Box 20683, Sedona, AZ 86341, (800) 244-1899. Though these bowls are specially "blessed," if you don't want the expense you could probably develop your own ritual to help you manifest your desires.

Facing Setbacks

Sometimes, in spite of our best efforts, we fail at something. Whether the setbacks are at work, in personal relationships, or finances, they are not the end of the world. If things have not turned out as planned, maybe even turned out badly, I say "Bravo!" At least you gave it a shot. The real failure in life is not in trying something that doesn't succeed, but in failing to try at all.

Anything we set out to do might fail. Nothing is risk-free. So accept that fact and continue on. Acknowledge that if failure happens, it is just another opportunity to learn what *not* to do next time. Learn how to re-define past failures as learning experiences and an adventure.

Exercise 8-5

Redefining "Failure"

as a *Learning Adventure*

My biggest "failure" in life has been:

As an important lesson in life, that "failure" successfully taught me the valuable lesson of:

Sometimes your actions don't succeed in one environment, but they would succeed in another. Given your personality, preferences, and work habits, you may want to consider changing jobs, or even cities, in order to succeed. If success doesn't seem likely in your current environment, find a more suitable environment. For example, if a job doesn't *feel* right, you know it. Seriously consider moving on. Think about the kind of environment and people you want in your life, then seek out that kind of life.

Prayer and Meditation

Studies have shown that prayer and meditation help cure illnesses, not just in ourselves but in others who are the subject of our prayers. Add prayer or meditation to your daily routine, not just to help cure depression, but to help you find guidance in all of your activities, and to help you stay centered and true to your ideals. You may even want to create your own prayer to recite on a regular basis which captures the essence of your thoughts and needs. Write it down, keep it with you, and recite it often.

Your Inner Voice: Friend or Foe?

One of the most powerful ingredients for mental health is a positive, affirming inner voice. But most of us hear an endless barrage of negativity from our inner voices, which is very unfortunate.

Often the inner voice is a series of negative questions such as "How come I never have enough money?" or "Why do I have to be so fat?" Or perhaps your voice is full of worry: "What if I mess up this presentation and lose my job?" If your head is full of questions like that, it's no wonder that you may feel out of control of your life.

Several years ago I was plagued by a series of inner voice messages that had me in a constant state of worry. Realizing I had to get a handle on the situation, I decided to write down a list of everything that was worrying me. Then I looked at the list, and it wasn't nearly as intimidating on paper as it had been when it was whirling around inside my head. The list had several things on it that were completely out of my control, such as my fear that my ten year old car would finally need to be junked, and I'd have to start making new car payments on my already-tight budget. I finally realized that the car was going to do what the car was going to do. It was out of my control, and worrying about it would not change the situation one bit. So I decided to stop worrying about it. Within a year, the car did give out and I somehow managed new car payments. But at least I didn't waste any energy worrying about something that I couldn't change.

The first thing you should do is determine what your inner voice is telling or asking you. Whatever your mind is fixated on is the problem you must endeavor to solve. After you have identified your old message, you can begin to replace it with new messages.

Figure 8-1

Inner Voice Examples

Old Messages	New Messages
Why am I so fat? Why can't I lose weight?	What low-calorie, nutritious food will be on my menu today? How many fruits and vegetables can I eat today? How much exercise can I get today?
Why can't I find my soulmate? Why do my relationships always fail?	How can I trust my instincts to be receptive and alert to my soul mate, and know which people to avoid? How can I be more loving, and find someone worthy of my love? What can I learn from my past relationships about the kind of characteristics I am looking for in a mate, and about the kind I wish to avoid? What good traits do I have to bring to a relationship?
Why am I always so broke?	How frugal can I be today? How can I learn to treat my money more wisely? What wasteful purchasing habits can I eliminate? How can I make it fun to stick to my budget? How can I learn more about investment strategies?

Old Messages	New Messages
Why is life so hard?	What can I do to help others less fortunate? How can I learn to better appreciate the gifts life has given me?
What if I lose my job?	What skills can I learn at this job that will prepare me for a better job in the future? How can I become more adaptive to change?

By creating a new set of messages that you would like to hear every day, you can train your inner voice to be your friend instead of your enemy. You can use these new messages to redirect your thoughts and actions to a more positive outcome.

Stop now and take ten minutes in *Exercise 8-5* to write down the negative messages you commonly receive from your inner voice. Take another twenty minutes to develop your list of positive new messages.

Then write the new messages on 3" x 5" cards and carry a copy with you, post a copy on your bathroom mirror, and keep a copy in your office desk drawer so you can refer to it often. After a few days or weeks of referring to the list, you will find yourself asking those new questions automatically, and be pleasantly surprised how it is affecting your attitude and behavior for the better.

Exercise 8-5

❦ Personal Plan to Change My Inner Voice ❦

My Old Messages	My New Messages

For further help in ridding your head of negative thoughts, here are a few more recommended books:

Build Your Own Road, Louis Wolf-Morgan
Choices, Shad Helmstetter
How to Stop Worrying and Start Living, Dale Carnegie
When All You've Ever Wanted Isn't Enough, Harold Kushner
How to Have More in a Have-Not World, Terry Cole-Whittaker
Negaholics: How to Overcome Negativity and Turn Your Life Around, Cherie Carter-Scott

Developing Other Interests

Depression can make you feel like nothing in the world is going right. Intellectually, you know that is not true, but emotionally you just aren't feeling good about anything. At that point, you are very narrowly focused on your own life, and don't see yourself as part of a bigger picture or useful or valuable to humanity in general. This chapter will address ways that you can find some new meaning in your life, if only in very small ways.

Most happy people have a variety of interests in their lives. They don't have just one thing going for them, they usually have several. Good relationships, satisfying jobs, comfortable (if modest) homes, good health, meaningful volunteer work, and interesting hobbies. Recent studies show that being well-rounded is good for your physical and mental health.

Hobbies provide a great deal of satisfaction. Some people pursue their hobbies with a passion and find real emotional fulfillment with the activities that fill their spare time. Think of all the freedom and happiness than can be derived from hobbies. Hobbies allow us to be one hundred percent creative, an opportunity which we can rarely find in our jobs. We can concentrate on "doing the right thing," a practice which is not welcomed in all work environments. (Imagine the distraught souls who lobby for the tobacco industries or pollute the environment in order to put food on the table for their families, while hating what their employer does for a profit and the role they play in the process.)

When we are engaged in our hobbies and volunteer work, we can work at our own pace, be it fast as lightening or slow as molasses. We can direct our energy as we see fit. We can learn and grow in areas that are of true interest to us. We can call it quits for the day whenever we want. We can share our work products with others. We can follow our dreams. We may be able to earn some extra income and there may even be some income tax benefits, depending on the latest tax reform legislation. All in all, hobbies and volunteerism are great ways to add meaning and value to our lives. It's a simple equation: Do something of value and you will be someone of value.

Some of you readers may think that you have no time for hobbies or volunteer work. But ask yourself these questions:

* How much television do I watch on a typical evening?

* How many hours does that add up to in a year (multiply by 365)?

* How have I benefited from all of those hours in front of the television?

If you are honest with yourself, you will acknowledge that most of that time in front of the television was wasted.

Do you, like so many of us, find yourself caught in the trap of "I'll-just-catch-the-evening-news-but-before-I-know-it-it's-eleven-o'clock-and-time-to-go-to-bed" syndrome? Don't be ashamed to admit it. But do be ashamed if you don't try to do something more productive with the time. This book was written at nights and on weekends over a period of more than two years. That was time that I might otherwise have spent watching television. I offer that as an example of how a few hours here and there can accumulate to result in an accomplished project.

Learn Something New

Perhaps some of your depression can be traced back to the fact that you are in a rut. Your days have been virtually identical for months or years. Nothing new has happened. Well, guess whose fault that is.

There are limitless opportunities to learn. Never in the history of humankind has there been more information available to more people at such little cost. Libraries are free and full of information on many topics you would find of interest. Local colleges and universities are conducting classes and one-day seminars. You could work on a new degree, or just take some fun continuing education classes. Some of these activities could work as joint activities for parents and children.

Think of the possibilities:

Acting
Foreign languages
Photography
Nutrition
First Aid/CPR
Computer Skills
Art
History
Cake Decorating
Catering
Woodworking
Cooking
Writing
Self-defense
Interior Design
Gardening
Crafts
Literature
Jewelry making

Serving Others

There is a world of opportunity to serve your church, community, the animal kingdom, or the planet. Volunteerism not only helps others, but it enriches your own life.

My father has been devoted to volunteerism all his life. When my sister and I were younger, Dad would bring us with him when he prepared and delivered Christmas baskets of food and toys for the needy in the back woods of northern Florida, a project of the local chapter of the International Lions Club. Those families were very poor, and were extremely grateful to have some food to put on the table at Christmas. The two dollar toy we brought might be the only toy their child received that year. Mothers often had tears in their eyes as they accepted their packages. Those trips not only gave my sister and I some lifelong memories of how good it feels to help others, but we also gained a greater appreciation for our own good fortune. We were of modest means, but compared to those poor families we had infinite riches.

Consider contributing your time to:

AIDS Babies
Big Brothers/Big Sisters
Drug Abuse Prevention
Citizen Watch Programs
Domestic Violence Prevention
Literacy Programs

Park and playground projects
Community Theater or Symphony
Nursing Home Visitation Programs
Environmental causes
Special Olympics

If you can't find a group you want to join, you can operate on your own or form an organization to fill an unmet need in your community. *Exercise 8-7* will help you identify a direction for your volunteer activities and hobbies. This is also a great thing to do with your kids. Volunteering builds character and expands horizons.

Exercise 8-7

❦ Personal Plan for Outside Interests ❦

My ideas for possible volunteer activities:

How many hours per week could I contribute?

Could my children participate with me?

My ideas for new hobbies or projects:

I am interested in learning more about:

What next steps should I take to follow through on the ideas above?

Chapter Nine: Eliminating Negative Influences

There are many factors that could be contributing, at least in a small way, to your depression. By identifying those contributing factors, you can gain more control over your mental attitude.

Medication Side Effects

You should research the side-effect of all of your medication, both prescription and over-the-counter (OTC) drugs such as antihistamines and sleeping pills. There are many books on the market which provide this information, and are easy for laypersons to understand. One such book is *The Pill Book*, an inexpensive paperback available in many bookstores.

If depression is listed among the side-effects of your medication, ask your doctor about alternative drug therapies or reduced dosages. Oral contraceptives are among the most commonly used prescription drugs which can have depression as a side-effect. If your drugs are deemed to be necessary, then you simply must be more committed to taking other actions, such as the ones outlined in this book, which will help to reduce the chances of depression.

Another aspect of drug side-effects is the unknown effects of combining drugs used for different purposes. There has been relatively little testing on drug interactions, and in many cases, doctors may be "flying blind" when prescribing a combination of drugs to their patients to treat various ailments. Ask your doctor about the known effects of mixing together the drugs that you are being prescribed. If they assure you that there is no problem mixing the drugs, ask him where he obtained that information, and if you could get a copy of any documentation. Such a request should prevent your questions from being "blown off" and not considered seriously. Your doctor may even appreciate your taking an interest in your prescriptions, because it indicates that you are willing to take some responsibility for your own health. I imagine he or she is tired of seeing patients who treat their bodies poorly and then unrealistically expect their doctors to repair all of their self-inflicted damage.

Illness Side Effects

Some illnesses can have depression as a side effect. Ask your health practitioner about the possible linkage, and try to learn more about how to treat those illnesses.

One of the most surprising linkages to me was candida (yeast infection), suffered by many women (and men, though less frequently), and which has depression as a common side effect. The good news is that candida is easily treated at the source, though not all doctors seem to be aware of quite how to do it. The most common medical treatment for these infections is the use of messy creams. Unfortunately, with this treatment, the infections tend to recur because creams treat only the symptom, not the source of the problem. Here are a few key points for sufferers of candida:

- It originates in the digestive system, as a result of bacterial imbalances.

- It is often brought on by the use of antibiotics.

- It can be aggravated by the consumption of too much sugary foods, carbonated beverages, and yeasty-foods, such as bread. (Ironically, those are the very foods that sufferers may crave at the time when they need them the least.)

- It may be relieved with the consumption of acidophilus (good bacteria), pau d'arco (an herb), and unsweetened yogurt.

Seasonal Affected Disorder (SAD)

By now, you have likely heard of the condition known as SAD, which tends to strike in the winter months, when daylight is shorter and the days are more gloomy. Many people suffering from SAD have found relief with daily exposure to artificial full-spectrum lighting. It replicates the light spectrums found in natural sunlight. Full spectrum lights are special light bulbs that can be used in your existing light sockets. Other configurations I have seen include what I would call "walls of light" that are more cumbersome and more likely to be used in severe cases of SAD.

Sources of full spectrum lighting are becoming more readily available, and you may be able to find full spectrum light bulbs in you local hardware store or health food store. Mail order suppliers include:

American Environmental Products
625 Mathews Street
Fort Collins, CO 80524
(800) 864-3883/(970) 493-6914 Fax

Chromalux
c/o Lumiram Corporation
PO Box 297
Mamaroneck, NY 10543
(914) 698-1205/(914) 698-5468 Fax
(800) 354-5596

Life Stages

Some stages of life may contribute to depression. It is important to remember that "This too shall pass."

Adolescence. Pre-teens and teens certainly do not have an easy time: peer pressure to participate in unwise or harmful activities, their body's hormonal changes, and academic stresses all challenge young people's ability to maintain their mental equilibrium, or positive mental attitude. At this age, learning about how to maintain a proper balance of mind/body/spirit can help youths cope with all the issues they must face as they grow up.

Young Adulthood. Young adults, especially women, can be particularly prone to depression. I suspect that some day science will find a hormonal contributing factor. But in our twenties and early thirties we undergo many stresses: new financial responsibilities, new career stress, and relationship stress. These are also the years where we are trying to figure out what we want to be when we grow up, and we think we had better hurry and be a success at it. We make mistakes because we are not yet wise, and we have not yet learned how to put our problems in the proper perspective. At this stage in life, it is important to face our problems and fears, believe in ourselves, get lots of exercise, and rely on our abilities and our faith to get us through life's inevitable difficulties.

Post-partum. Many new mothers experience periods of depression, and with good reason. Hormonal changes, childbirth pain, adjustment to a new family member who is one hundred percent dependent, sleepless nights, and additional housework (often with little help from their spouse or significant other). In these cases, mothers should try to get some time to themselves, try to enjoy their new baby, and stop trying to be supermom. Make sure you maintain a good nutrition and exercise regimen, and you will be feeling better soon.

Parenthood. Raising a child is an incredibly stressful job and more children mean more stress. Each child needs attention, love, direction, monitoring, guidance --- not to mention food, clean clothes, baths, and help with homework. Stay-at-home parents get little or no relief until children are old enough to go to school for a few hours a day. It will be a challenge, but try to be creative and incorporate your children into as many recommendations in this book as possible. Ask for help when you need it. Try to form a neighborhood "time bank" where you take turns watching each others' children for a few hours at a time. Also, remember to stop and take deep breaths when you are feeling particularly stressed.

Menopause. One of the unfortunate side effects of the transitional life cycle of menopause is the possibility of depression. The good news is that it should soon pass. In the meantime, one of the best treatments is Siberian ginseng, as is discussed elsewhere in this book. Exercise is also highly recommended. Many of the treatments that help treat depression are also useful in helping women deal with other physical effects of menopause.

Seniors. Depression is not uncommon among senior citizens. They may have lost many of their closest friends, been moved from their homes into nursing facilities, be less physically active, and/or be suffering side effects of medications. This group should get regular exercise, eat a well-balanced diet, and try many of the other natural remedies suggested in this book. The good news is that seniors are usually retired, and have more time to follow-up on the various strategies to treat depression, so that the years ahead can still be happy and rewarding.

Smoking

Smoking and its toxins may be contributing to your depression, but even if it is not, you should stop smoking -- for the sake of your loved ones as well as yourself. Smoking (and second hand smoke) can cause cancer, asthma, a host of other health problems. If that's not enough to make you stop, remember that it also causes wrinkles.

In the mid-1990's Hollywood began to re-glamorize smoking both cigarettes and cigars, in film and on magazine covers. Movie stars and other celebrities who have participated in this campaign should be ashamed of themselves for encouraging others to adopt this deadly habit. Don't be fooled by the hype -- smoking can ruin your health.

Food Allergies

Many people suffer from food allergies without realizing it. Some of the most common food allergies are to dairy products, meat, wheat, and sweeteners. These allergies may manifest themselves in many ways including digestive problems, rashes, and depression. Odds are slim that food allergies have single-handedly triggered your depression, but food allergies can make an ongoing episode of depression more severe or simply help to maintain a low-grade depression.

To test yourself for food allergies, try a fruit and vegetable diet for two to three weeks. Then gradually reintroduce dairy products into your diet. Do you notice any changes in your mood? Gradually introduce meats, wheat, and sweeteners, noting any impact of each on your mood. The chances that you have some degree of food allergy are probably greater than you think. If you go through the above exercise and you can't find a linkage to your depression, you may find other benefits of isolating a food allergy, such as improved digestion or skin appearance.

Toxins

Since toxins are poisons to the body, it is best to eliminate as many as possible. This will help maximize your physical health - which impacts your mental health.

Common toxins include the pesticides used in farming our foods, air pollution, and water pollution. (I recently saw a scary story on national news about sludge that was too toxic to be dumped in our water supply, so it was renamed "fertilizer" and is now being used on our nations food crops! That story certainly motivated me to go out of my way to shop for untainted, organic foods.) A few simple steps can reduce or eliminate toxins in your life:

* buy only organically-grown foods,

* get more fresh air by using good air filters in your home and keeping green plants indoors, and

* drink lots of bottled or filtered water to help flush the toxins out of your system.

Electromagnetic Fields and Waves

Electromagnetic waves could be a contributing factor to depression because they are one more kind of toxin that your body must fight off. Though recent studies have discounted the possibility of harmful effects from high voltage power lines, I am not aware of any studies that have been conducted on long term (over five years) exposure (especially on children, who are more susceptible to any toxic agent).

Sources of electromagnetic fields (EMFs) include televisions, microwaves, computers, electric blankets, and electric clock radios. The good news is that the farther away we stand or sit from those sources, the effect of the waves is lessened. While you can't sit very far from your computer while you work on it, you can fit it with a radiation screen to drastically reduce the effects of the waves.

Negative Influences

Negative influences come in many forms: people (family, friends, co-workers), movies, and music. You can probably think of many other sources of negative energy, and it is important to identify these negative influences and reduce your exposure to them.

Any friend or family member who constantly criticizes you, discourages your dreams, and blocks your positive energy, does not have your best interest at heart (or at least doesn't know how to show it). Explain to them that you have decided to eliminate (or drastically reduce) their influence over you unless they become more loving and supportive, and promise to change your own behaviors toward them if you yourself have been an unsupportive friend. If they refuse to change, find new friends who are more encouraging and supportive. Minimize the time spent with those unsupportive family members, too, and try to let their destructive comments roll off your back.

Financial Difficulties

While the love of money may be the root of all evil, the lack of money may be the root of many people's depression. For most of us the problem is usually not in earning enough, but in living within our means or worrying about losing our jobs in a corporate downsizing, or "rightsizing."

The flash and excess of the 1980's taught many of us to value "things" over ideals. We showed our value by wearing expensive clothes, driving fancy cars, and eating out at trendy restaurants. And every month we worried about how to pay the bills as they came due. We know better now, but we are still paying for our misplaced values of the past.

If it has been more than ten years since your credit cards have seen a zero balance you are, in effect, still paying interest on clothes that you bought nine years ago and gave away to Goodwill three years ago. Even worse, years later you may still be paying for meals you charged at local restaurants that didn't stay in your system more than a few hours. (Well, some of it may still be on your hips, but that's a different issue.)

The point is, if you don't control your money, your money will control you. Being broke is no fun, and it can add an enormous amount of unneeded stress to your life. As we approach the millennium, we can learn from the religious orders of the monks, the philosophies of the East, and even the less materialistic X-Generation. Find happiness in who you are, not in what you own.

Here are some tips for getting your financial life in order.

* Don't charge purchases on credit cards. Pay cash for all your purchases except your car and your home.

* Don't buy anything on impulse, no matter how inexpensive. Go home and think about it for at least 24 hours. Longer, if a lot of money is at stake. Enlist the aid of your friends and family who may shop with you.

* Do pay off high-interest credit card debt. Take out a home equity loan (interest then becomes tax-deductible) or shift to a credit card with a lower interest rate. If you have a good payment history, your current credit

card company may even lower its rate if you threaten to move your business.

* Don't shop as a form of entertainment. If you shop for sport or pleasure, you definitely need another hobby. If you have "shopping buddies," try meeting for tea or volunteer work instead. Find another activity to do together that is less expensive and/or more productive. Also, remember than the little purchases add up to large amounts. If you spend $8 per day on lunch at work, that adds up to $2,000 per year. Three dollars per day spent on snacks and sodas, that's $750. And if you eat dinner out twice a week at $40 per meal, that's $4,160.

* Do start saving on a regular basis. Payroll deduction plans are great because the money goes straight into savings before you have the opportunity to touch it. Save for short term emergency needs and for retirement. You'll get an extra boost if your employer matches your savings. The earlier you start saving, the more comfortable your retirement will be. It's never to early to start saving for retirement -- even if you are

in your twenties. Millionaire status is *very* possible if you start that early!!! Set a savings target of five to ten percent of your salary.

* Do learn more about money and investments, and about controlling your attitude about money. Read magazines and books that will teach you about money management.

* Do learn to manage your taxes. You will spend more of your lifetime earnings on taxes than on housing. Stay current on changes in the tax law with books published annually by reputable sources. There is no need to accidentally pay more in taxes than you are legally required to pay. Before you get married, talk to a tax professional -- especially if you are a professional couple or you own real estate. That's when tax laws are especially unfair and must be navigated carefully.

* Don't buy to impress others. Earn the respect and admiration of your friends and peers in other ways. (If they are only impressed with material things, are they really the kind of people you want as friends?)

* Do keep learning new job skills so that you will always be employable, no matter what happens with any particular job. Be committed to "lifelong learning" -- and enjoy the process.

* Do make a budget and stick to it. Decide how much money should be spent on various expense categories (housing, groceries, clothes, entertainment, savings, etc.).

* Do find inexpensive ways to have fun with friends and loved ones. Replace fancy restaurant meals with home-made pasta dinners. Skip the movie theater and wait for the video. Plan a picnic in the park.

* Do be generous with those less fortunate. If you can't afford financial gifts, donate some of your time.

Take time to determine your current financial status. The best way might be to prepare a personal balance sheet. The concept is simple. A balance sheet is a listing of the value of the things you own (assets), and a listing of how much you owe (liabilities). The difference between the two is your personal net worth. Use the example to prepare your own in *Exercise 9-1*:

Figure 9-1

Sample Balance Sheet

Assets	
Cash in checking account	$ 75
Cash in savings account	1,000
Stocks	1,000
Retirement savings	7,000
Car	14,000
House	90,000
Total Assets	$113,075
Liabilities	
Credit Cards	$ 1,500
Car Loan	13,000
Mortgage	80,000
Total Liabilities	$ 94,500
Net Worth (calculated as assets minus liabilities)	$ 18,575
Total Liabilities and Net Worth (Notice how the total equals, or "balances," with the assets; hence the term Balance Sheet.)	$ 113,075

Exercise 9-1

Personal Balance Sheet

Assets	
Cash in checking account	$
Cash in savings account	
Stocks	
Retirement savings	
Cars	
House	
Other:	
Total Assets	$
Liabilities	
Credit Cards	$
Car Loans	
Mortgage	
Total Liabilities	$
Net Worth (total assets minus total liabilities)	$
Total Liabilities and Net Worth	$

Don't be surprised if you find that your net worth is less than you thought. You may even find that you have a negative net worth -- meaning that you owe more than you own. Consider this your wake-up call. In order for you to feel financially secure, you need to increase your cash balances and net worth. Set some financial goals for the next six months, one year, five year, and ten year time frames. How much money do you want to have in your retirement funds? How much do you want to owe? Do you want to pay off your mortgage early? Establish college funds for your children? How much do you want to be worth in ten years?

By establishing your financial goals, you can be more focused on the direction you are headed. Identifying the steps needed to reach your financial goals is another topic entirely, one that we won't address in this book. But there are some fabulous books and magazines on the market that can teach you how to reach those goals.

Here are just a few of the books and magazines that I recommend for readers who are ready to get their financial house in order:

* *Kiplinger's Personal Finance Magazine* (800) 544-0155,

* *Money Magazine* (800) 633-9970,

* *The Truth About Money*, by Ric Edelman, Georgetown University Press, 1996,

* *The Five Rituals of Wealth*, by Tod Barnhart, Harper Business, 1995, and

* *Your Money or Your Life*, by Joe Dominguez and Vicki Robin, Penguin Books, 1992.

Job Stress

These days, job stress may be at the root of many people's depression. Jobs are no longer secure, no matter how hard we work, or how talented we are. Most of us have financial responsibilities beyond ourselves; other people (our families) are counting on our paycheck to keep them fed and sheltered. We feel compelled to work long hours, usually for little or no extra reward, so that if the ax falls -- maybe it will fall on the next person instead because he didn't work as hard as we did.

But we may be stressed not only by the amount of work we are expected to do, or the threat of imminent job loss. Often, we have jobs that do not seem to match up well with our true interests and passions. In fact, we may be working for an employer that is damaging the health of the planet and its people, and our soul can only ignore that truth for just so long.

Our jobs define who we are to a large degree, fortunately or unfortunately. If we don't like the person that we have become at our job, we must take action and make changes. We must work toward a job that fulfills both our emotional and financial needs. We must enjoy what we do for a living.

Many people who are "downsized" are traumatized at first, but later say that it was the best thing that ever happened to them. It forced them to re-evaluate their career choices, and to choose a new path that was more emotionally, and often financially, rewarding. It is important to find work that you are passionate about. In any field, there are people who truly love what they do, so you can be sure they will be among the best in their field. And you will be competing with them. So it only makes sense to be one of those people who are passionate about their work.

One of the most important things you can do for your mental health is to find a mission in life that is the embodiment of your ideals, and that inspires you with passion. The hardest thing, however, may be to find your mission. Keep in mind that it may not be any one thing. It may be a series of things that link with each other as you progress through your life. Making the transition from work that you do to work that you love is not likely to be easy. For financial security, you may want to pursue your life's mission on a part-time basis, keeping your full-time job to build your financial security, or even fund your start-up operation. That is the strategy that many new entrepreneurs follow.

There are some great books on the market that can help lead you along the path of discovery as you search for your mission, and help you with practical aspects of resume writing and interviewing. Those books, like this one, require action on your part. You must work through the exercises, and really think long and hard as you work through the processes of uncovering your true mission in life. Recommended books include:

* *What Color Is Your Parachute?* by Richard Bolles (updated annually),

* *Zen and the Art of Making a Living*, by Lawrence G. Boldt, Penguin Group, 1993,

* *Change Your Job/Change Your Life*, by Ronald L. Krannich, Ph.D., Impact Publications, 1995, and

* *Do What You Love and the Money Will Follow: Discovering Your Right Livelihood*, by Marsha Sinetar, Dell Publishing, 1987.

Women, in particular, may find job stress to be a contributing factor to their depression. Studies have shown that women and men tend to react differently to success and failure at work. When successful, men take personal credit; women credit good luck. When things go wrong, men blame external factors; women blame themselves. Regardless of your sex, take care not to let your job success or failure define your value as a person. Your job is just one aspect of a well-balanced life.

In order to keep our job in the proper perspective, we sometimes have to step away from it. Vacations are very important to our mental health, and it is important to take a vacation that is worlds away (at least psychologically) from our work. Be sure and plan for one or two great vacations a year, with some mini-vacations throughout the year. Even a one-day visit to a mini-spa can help keep you emotionally balanced.

Whatever the ultimate reason for our job stress, we are not without options. We make choices every day, whether we realize it or not. We choose to get out of bed, get dressed, and go to work. We chose whether or not to let problems upset us. We could also chose to address our job stress issues in a mature, professional way. Take some time to consider how to best resolve your job stress issues.

Jealousy

Jealousy is a very harmful emotion that backfires on the perpetrator. It wastes a lot of energy and makes for bitterness and small-mindedness. Instead of being jealous of someone who has something that you want, reinterpret the situation.

Learn from them. What did they do to get where they are? Did they work harder? Make more sacrifices? Treat people differently?

Let's take an example. Everyone loves to hate Martha Stewart. She's rich, beautiful, successful, and the perfect hostess with the perfect house, her own television show, and magazine. Rather than envy her, why not think of her as a great role model? She works hard, believes in herself, and is very disciplined and organized. She has a keen entrepreneurial spirit, is a tough negotiator, and a marketing genius. And she has done it all on her own. Why not respect her and learn from her, rather than hate her for her accomplishments?

Sometimes people are jealous without realizing it, they just know that they dislike another person. Think about someone you dislike, and try to specify why you don't like them. If you can't think of a really good reason, you may simply be jealous of their looks, money, position, or job. I remember my first job after college, and how I had decided that I disliked a particular woman who worked there, before I had even met her. She was just too pretty; she looked like a human Barbie doll. Well, when I finally did meet her she turned out to be one of the nicest people I had ever met. She was smart, very down-to-earth, unassuming, and fun to be around. I realized that I had been a jerk, and I learned a very important lesson about jealousy.

Learn to turn that jealous negative energy into positive energy in *Exercise 9-2*. And stop being so catty. It makes you look bad.

Exercise 9-2

Learning Lessons from Jealousy

Name someone who makes you feel jealous.

What do they have that you want?

How did they achieve it?

How can you learn from the person who is the object of your jealousy?

Is it possible to become friends with that person, rather than remaining enemies, if such is the case?

Low Self-Esteem

Studies have shown that it is very important for people to like themselves; it is one of the key traits of happy people. And it makes perfect sense. How could you be a *totally* happy person if you didn't respect yourself or consider yourself a worthy person? How can the love you offer to others be of much value if you don't love yourself?

If you determine that you suffer from low self-esteem, try to determine its root cause. If a particular criticism has haunted you for years, refer to inner voice *Exercise 8-5*, and replace that criticism with a positive, reinforcing message.

If you don't like who you are, then decide who you want to be, and "Fake it 'til you make it." Select a personal hero and ask yourself what they would do in your situation to turn lemons into lemonade.

Identifying and Curbing Negative Influences

This chapter has identified an assortment of potential negative influences in your life. It is likely that you can identify even more. *Exercise 9-3* is intended to empower you to identify action steps that you can take to curb those negative influences. Sketch out your preliminary thoughts here in this book, but follow up with more detailed action plans on a larger piece of paper. Then follow through with those plans.

Exercise 9-3

❦ Personal Plan for Identifying Possible Negative Influences ❦

Possible Factor	Likely? (Y/N)	Action Plan
Medications		
Illnesses/Allergies		
Life Stage		
Smoking		
Electromagnetic Waves		
Negative Influences People Media		
Toxins		
Stresses Financial Job		
Jealousy/Self-Esteem		

❦❦❦

Chapter Ten: Developing Your Action Plan

The completion of this chapter will result in the culmination of all of your work in previous chapters. By now, you should have tested a number of the recommended remedies, and know which ones work for you.

This book has provided you with a multitude of easy, effective remedies to relieve and prevent depression. However, reading alone will not cure or prevent your depression. You need a plan of action with two parts: 1) a maintenance plan, to maintain a positive outlook and high energy level, and 2) an offensive strategy (or rescue plan) for rising above depression when it hits. I am convinced that the more seriously you stick to the maintenance plan, the less often you will need to go on the offensive to combat a case of depression.

The Maintenance Plan

A maintenance plan is your prevention plan, your long-term strategy for maintaining happiness. It should provide a nice balance of nutrients, beneficial herbs, positive environment, and activities. Some should be a part of your daily life, others are needed less frequently. A sample maintenance plan is presented in *Figure 10-1*. You will be applying that concept to develop your own personal maintenance plan could adapting it to your own purposes, interests, and lifestyle. If you religiously adhere to a maintenance plan, you may have little need to ever use your rescue plan.

Figure 10-1

Sample Maintenance Plan

Daily	1 -3 Times Weekly	1 - 4 Times Monthly	1 - 4 Times Annually
Vitamins B-complex C Iron Ginko Biloba Ginseng Healthy Diet Deep Breaths	Herbal teas Upbeat music Exercise Aromatherapy bath Prayer Hobby Focus on Life's mission	Nature Walk Massage Volunteer Class Read health magazines	Vacation Spa

The Rescue Plan

The rescue plan is your short-term plan to relieve depression when it hits. It steps up the frequency of many items in the maintenance plan, and may also incorporate some additional items that did not make it onto your maintenance plan. A sample intensive rescue plan is presented in *Figure 10-2*.

The reason for a rescue plan is simple. If you have a plan, you won't panic if you develop a sudden case of depression. You can calmly work your way through the list of activities, nutrients, and other remedies until you achieve relief. You will have taken control of the situation, and will be busy working your plan, with the understanding that you will need patience until things are back to normal. When the episode has passed, you can revert back to your maintenance plan.

Figure 10-2

❦ Sample Rescue Plan ❦

Daily	1 -3 Times Weekly	1 - 4 Times Monthly	1 - 4 Times Annually
Vitamins B-complex C Iron Ginko Biloba Ginseng St. Johns Wort Green tea AM Chamomile tea PM Healthy Diet Deep Breaths Full spectrum lighting Nature walk Prayer Upbeat music Exercise Smile-in-the-Box	Aromatherapy bath Hobby Communicate with friends/ family Visualization	Nature Walk Massage Volunteer Class	Vacation Spa

Your Personal Plans

Now, it is time to create your own maintenance and rescue plans in *Exercises 10-1* and *10-2*, based on your notes from earlier chapters, outside reading, or any other source that has given you ideas. Keep a copy with you at all times for reference, and to help keep you disciplined. You may want to use a separate, larger piece of paper, or change the frequency of the column headings.

Exercise 10-1

Your Personal Maintenance Plan

Daily	1 -3 Times Weekly	1 - 4 Times Monthly	1 - 4 Times Annually

Exercise 10-2

Your Personal Rescue Plan

Daily	1 -3 Times Weekly	1 - 4 Times Monthly	1 - 4 Times Annually

Phone numbers of supportive friends:

Favorite inspirational reading passages:

Favorite uplifting music:

I encourage you to make copies of your rescue and maintenance plans and keep them with you. During a period of depression, refer to the list several times a day to make sure you are sticking to your plan, and doing everything you know to do so that you can start feeling better sooner. You may also want to figure out how you can best include your plan in your calendar or day planner.

As part of your maintenance plan I encourage you to continue to learn about natural ways to maintain your physical and mental health. One easy way is to subscribe to a good magazine dedicated to natural health, and the mail can bring frequent news updates and information to you. These magazines cover a broad range of health issues for men, women, and children. Several very good magazines include:

Natural Health (Excellent!!)	(800) 526-8440
New Age Journal	(617) 926-0200
Mothering	(800) 984-8116
HerbalGram	(512) 331-8868
Alternative Medicine Digest	(800) 515-HEAL
Yoga Journal	(800) 334-8152

If you have a General Nutrition Center (GNC) in your area, it's a good idea to become a Gold Card member. You'll receive discounts, and a free subscription to *Let's Live*. (This is true at the time of this writing, anyway.) Other local health food stores or co-ops may have similar discount programs.

Beware of magazines with too many advertisements for pharmaceutical drugs. They are not going to be truly dedicated to providing you with the latest unbiased information on natural health, if their revenues are heavily dependent on pharmaceutical advertising dollars.

Conclusion

By the time you have worked your way to the end of this book, you should have gained a level of confidence in your ability to control your moods, attitudes, energy, and thoughts. You have learned how to gradually put feelings of hopelessness and despair behind you while you build a renewed appreciation for life's pleasures and wonders, and your opportunities to love, learn, and grow.

You have learned some basic lessons on achieving a healthy state of balance in mind, body, and spirit. You know to be more thoughtful and deliberate about how you live your life:

* the foods, beverages and nutritional supplements you consume,
* the level of physical activity you need,
* the quality and quantity of time spent in meditation, prayer, and relaxation,
* the amount of time spent interacting with nature,
* the degree to which you train your mind to ask the right questions,

* your focus on goals and mission,

* your ability to limit negative influences and increase your exposure to positive influences, and

* your commitment maintain a lifestyle that reinforces your natural state of balance and happiness.

As your new choices become habits, a healthy lifestyle will seem almost effortless. Not only will you be a happier person, but you will set an example for others who see changes in you that they would like to replicate in their own lives. Then the student can become the teacher.

As you continue your journey through life, you will encounter new ideas that you can incorporate into a lifestyle that will further nourish your growing sense of happiness and serenity. Feel free to modify your plan with new ideas, or to meet changing circumstances. Just remember that your plan must address the mental, physical, and spiritual components of good health. Balance of those three aspects of your life is essential for long term success.

Now go forward, feeling empowered to live the kind of life you have envisioned for yourself. You now know what it takes to nurture happiness in your life. Sow those seeds, and reap those rewards. You deserve to be happy.

Bibliography and Reference

Atwood, Mary Dean. *Spirit Healing: Native American Magic & Medicine.* New York: Sterling Publishing Co., 1991.

Balch, James F., M.D., and Balch, Phyllis A. C.N.C. *Prescription for Nutritional Healing.* Garden City Park, NY: Avery Publishing Group, Inc., 1990.

Barendsen, Kristin. "Healing From Depression," *Yoga Journal*, December 1996. Escondido, CA. California Yoga Teachers Association. pp. 44 - 141.

Barone, Don and Faelten, Sharon. Tkac, Debora, ed. *LifeSpan-Plus* (By the Editors of PREVENTION Magazine). New York: MJF Books, 1990.

Bergner, Paul. *The Healing Power of Garlic: The Enlightened Person's Guide to Nature's Most Versatile Medicinal Plant.* Rocklin, California: Prima Publishing, 1996.

Bergner, Paul. *The Healing Power of Ginsing and the Tonic Herbs: The Enlightened Person's Guide.* Rocklin, California: Prima Publishing, 1996.

Bock, Steven J., M.D. and Boyette, Michael. *Stay Young the Melatonin Way.* New York: Penguin Press, 1995.

Brody, Jane. *Jane Brody's Nutrition Book.* New York: W.W. Norton and Company, 1981.

Challem, Jack. "Health Brief: DHEA," *Natural Health Magazine*, Vol. 26, No. 6, November/December 1996.

Coggins, Kip. *Alternative Pathways to Healing: The Recovery Medicine Wheel.* Deerfield Beach, Florida: Health Communications, Inc. 1990.

Crook, William G., M.D. *The Yeast Connection: A Medical Breakthrough.* Jackson, TN: Professional Books, 1985.

Chopra, Deepak, M.D. *Ageless Body, Timeless Mind.* New York: Harmony Books, 1993.

Curtis, Susan and Fraser, Romy. *Natural Healing for Women.* London, Pandora Press, 1991.

Diamond, Harvey and Harvey, Marilyn. *Fit for Life II: Living Health.* New York: Warner Books, 1989.

Dobelis, Inge N., ed. *Magic and Medicine of Plants.* Pleasantville, NY: The Reader's Digest Association, Inc., 1989.

Eades, Mary Dan, M.D. *The Doctor's Complete Guide to Vitamins and Minerals.* New York: Dell Publishing, 1994.

Geller, Jeffrey L. and Harris, Maxine. *Women of the Asylum: Voices from Behind the Walls 1840-1945.* New York: Anchor Books, 1994.

Gordon, James S., M.D. *Manifesto for a New Medicine: Your Guide to Healing Partnerships and the Wise Use of Alternative Therapies.* Reading, Massachusetts: Addison-Wesley Publishing Co., Inc., 1996.

Grauds, Constance E., RPh. "Brain Boosting Herbs," *Veggie Life Magazine,* March 1997.

Grieve, Mrs. M. *A Modern Herbal.* Kent: Dorset Press, 1994.

Griffith, H. Winter, M.D. *Complete Guide to Vitamins, Minerals, and Supplements.* Tuscon, Arizona: Fisher Books, 1988.

Hogarth, Michael, M.D. and Hutchinson, David, R.N. *An Internet Guide for the Health Professional.* Sacramento, California: New Wind Publishing, 1996.

Kamen, Betty, Ph.D. *Siberian Ginseng: Up-to-Date Research on the Fabled Oriental Tonic Herb.* New Canaan, CT: Keats Publishing, Inc., 1988.

Kingston, Karen. *Creating Sacred Space with Feng Shui: Learn the Art of Space Clearing and*

Bring New Energy into Your Life. New York: Broadway Books, 1997.

Lawless, Julia. *The Illustrated Encyclopedia of Essential Oils.* Rockport, MA: Element Books, 1995.

Lim, Robin. *After the Baby's Birth ... A Woman's Way to Wellness.* Berkeley, CA: Celestial Arts, 1991.

Lust, John. *The Herb Book.* New York: Bantam Books, 1974.

Matthews, Andrew. *Being Happy! A Handbook to Greater Confidence and Security.* New York: Price Stern Sloan, Inc., 1990.

Mayell, Mark. *Off-the-Shelf Natural Health: How to Use Herbs and Nutrients to Stay Well.* New York: Bantam Books, 1995.

McGilvery, Carole, and Reed, Jimi. *Essential Aroma-therapy.* New York: SMITHMARK Publishers, Inc., 1994.

Mead, Nathaniel. "Health Brief: Milk Thistle," *Natural Health Magazine*, May-June 1997.

Melody. *Love Is In The Earth: A Kaleidoscope of Crystals.* Updated. Wheat Ridge, Colorado: Earth-Love Publishing House, 1995.

Mindell, Dr. Earl. *What You Should Know About the Super Antioxidant Miracle.* New Canaan, Connecticut: Keats Publishing, Inc., 1996.

Murray, Michael, N.D., and Pizzorno, Joseph, N.D. *Encyclopedia of Natural Medicine.* Rocklin, CA: Prima Publishing. 1991.

Northrup, Christiane, M.D. "Woman to Woman," *Natural Health Magazine*, February 1997.

Null, Dr. Gary. *The Woman's Encyclopedia of Natural Healing: The New Healing Techniques of 100 Leading Alternative Health Practitioners.* New York: Seven Stories Press, 1996.

"Prozac is Not Infant-Friendly; A Mother's Use Can Lead to a Baby's Defects," *Alterntive Medicine Digest*, Issue 17, March/April 1997.

Redwood, Daniel, D.C. *Edgar Cayce's Holistic Health Program: The Amazing Mind/Body/Spirit Approach of America's Most Famous Healer.* New Canaan, Connecticut: Keats Publishing, Inc., 1996.

Robbins, John. *Diet for a New America: How Food Choices Affect Your Health, Happiness and the Future of Life on Earth.* Walpole, New Hampshire: Stillpoint Publishing, 1987.

Robbins, John. *Reclaiming Our Health.* Tiburon, CA: HJKramer, Inc., 1996.

Sachs, Judith. "Nature's Prozac: A Better Way to Treat Depression and Panic Attacks," *Let's Live Magazine*, Vol. 65, No. 4, April 1997.

Sahelian, Ray, M.D. "Anti-Aging Update," *Let's Live Magazine*, Vol. 65, No. 4, April 1997.

Sellar, Wanda. *The Directory of Essential Oils.* Essex: C.W. Daniel Company Limited, 1993.

Silverman, Harold M., ed. *The Pill Book.* New York: Bantam Books, 1994.

Somer, Elizabeth, M.A., R.D. *Food & Mood.* New York, Henry Holt and Company, 1996.

Stein, Diane. *The Natural Remedy Book for Women. Freedom*, CA: The Crossing Press, 1995.

Tanouye, Elyse. "Antidepressant Makers Study Kids Market," *Wall Street Journal*, April 4, 1997: B1.

The Book of Tea and Herbs. Santa Rosa: The Cole Group, 1993.

Trowbridge, John Parks, M.D., and Walker, Morton, D.P.M. *The Yeast Syndrome.* New York: Bantam Books, 1986.

Walker, Barbara G. *The Book of Sacred Stones: Fact and Fallacy in the Crystal World.* San Francisco, Harper Collins, 1989.

Walker, Dr. Morton. *The Power of Color.* Garden City Park: Avery Publishing Group, Inc., 1991.

Weil, Andrew, M.D. *Natural Health, Natural Medicine.* New York: Houghton Mifflin, 1995.

Weil, Andrew, M.D. *Spontaneous Healing: How to Discover and Enhance Your Body's Natural Ability to Maintain and Heal Itself.* New York: Fawcett Columbine, 1995.

Williams, Dr. David G., ed. *Alternatives Newsletter.* Mountain Home Publishing, Kerville, Texas. March 1996.

Williams, Dr. David G. *Secrets of Supercharging Your Immune System the Natural Way.* Ingram, TX: Mountain Home Publishing, 1994.

Worwood, Valerie Ann. *The Fragrant Pharmacy: A Complete Guide to Aromatherapy & Essential Oils.* London: Bantam Books, 1993.

Yapko, Michael D., Ph. D. "The Art of Avoiding Depression," *Psychology Today*, Vol. 30, No. 3, May/June 1997.

Zimlicki, Paula M. "Deciphering DHEA," *New Age Journal*, January/February 1997.

ORDER FORM

I would like to order ____ (number) copies of *Nurturing Happiness: Natural Ways to Relieve and Prevent Depression* at $11.95 each.

Number of copies requested	
Times price per copy	$11.95
Subtotal	
VA residents add sales tax of 4.5%	
Plus shipping and handling of $3.00 per copy	
Total	

Please send check or money order to:

Windmill Press of Alexandria
PO Box 9161
Alexandria, VA 22304

Please inquire about quantity discounts.